ONCE UPON A LIFE

We know the past can be changed. We can choose what we should believe; we can choose what we should remember. This is what frees us, this choice, frees us to hope...

Amy Tan
The Opposite of Fate

ONCE UPON A LIFE
Burnt Curry and Bloody Rags

A Memoir

TEMSULA AO

zubaan

ZUBAAN
an imprint of Kali for Women
128B Shahpur Jat, 1st floor
NEW DELHI 110 049
Email: contact@zubaanbooks.com
Website: www.zubaanbooks.com

First published by Zubaan 2013

10 9 8 7 6 5 4 3 2 1

ISBN: 978 93 81017 98 2

Zubaan is an independent feminist publishing house based in New Delhi with a strong academic and general list. It was set up as an imprint of India's first feminist publishing house, Kali for Women, and carries forward Kali's tradition of publishing world quality books to high editorial and production standards. *Zubaan* means tongue, voice, language, speech in Hindustani. Zubaan is a non-profit publisher, working in the areas of the humanities, social sciences, as well as in fiction, general non-fiction, and books for children and young adults under its Young Zubaan imprint.

Typeset in ITC Veljovic Std 10/13 by Jojy Philip
Printed at Raj Press, R-3 Inderpuri, New Delhi 110 012

This book is dedicated
to the memory of my parents
Imnamathongba Changkiri
and
Nokyintemla Longkumer
and my brothers
Kharibong and Tajenyuba
and my sister
Sutsungkala

Preface

It has not been an easy task writing this book and the reader
will understand why as the story unfolds. But I have done it
because of certain inner compulsions.

The narratives in this book cover some of the most
significant incidents in the different phases of my life,
a life that went on to overcome the travails of a most
difficult childhood, early marriage and the subsequent
responsibilities of a single parent raising four children and
coping with the demands of a full-time job. The memories
of that life presented here are the most insistent ones which
depict the journey of an individual in search of the self-
worth once lost to time and circumstances. This book is
basically a memoir rather than an auto-biography because,
as Gore Vidal has said, '*A memoir is how one remembers one's
life, while an auto-biography is history, requiring research, dates
and facts double-checked*'. Therefore the accuracy required in
an auto-biography has not been attempted here; nor has any
chronological detail or sequence been mentioned or strictly
followed. The only principle adhered to here is the effort
to present the authenticity and intensity of the impressions
retained in the memory of a heart which has borne the
burden of an excruciating truth these many years with a

clarity and sharpness that have not been diluted or lessened by time.

At the most intimate and personal level, the book is an attempt to put a semblance of coherence and a sense of summation into the dialogue that I have been trying to have with my children over these long years, verbal or otherwise, in order to make them understand what has gone into the making of this imperfect woman whom they call mother. There were many times when my prattling about my own childhood as contrasted to theirs would evoke the response, 'Yes mommy, but those days were different'. At other times, I would be rebuffed by their silence; hurting inside, but unable to proceed further because I did not know how to penetrate the barrier of their youthful indifference. At times I even accused them inwardly of being insensitive and unfeeling.

But in spite of an uneasy and prolonged state of being in a parental limbo which became my lot, I persevered because I believed that I deserved to be heard and if verbal communication failed, then I had to leave them a legacy in writing which would make them appreciate what they are now and what they have had in terms of parental love and care. This is therefore an offering to my children, my version of the book of knowledge about ordinary lives: the joys and sorrows, about plenty and poverty and, most importantly, this book is about love and what it is like to be deprived of it.

At another level, it is an attempt to exorcise my own personal ghosts from a fractured childhood that was ripped apart by a series of tragedies. There is however no claim to exclusivity in the nature of deprivation and suffering that we had to go through because sufferings of children through natural catastrophes and other causes have been an inevitable ingredient of human history. But a story becomes unique when the sufferer survives to find a better future and lives to tell the story. That is why I consider it imperative that I tell my personal history so that the telling will heal some old wounds in an ageing heart. And if in the sharing a new response is generated in the minds of loved ones, I will consider it a just reward for living through the painful recollection.

But there is another important reason for writing this account: it has been prompted by a sense of wonder at our ultimate destinies; how from being absolute destitutes we were able to achieve a measure of success both as individuals of some personal merit and as decent members of society. Many others, family and friends alike, often express this sense of wonder at our ultimate fate. I remember an old aunt's comment when all six of us were well-settled in life. With a directness typical of rural folk but devoid of any malice, she said, 'By all human reckoning, you all should have been eating dust as beggars, or at best become menial servants in other people's houses. But look at you now, you all have made your way in the world and found your rightful places in society. Your lives are prime examples of God's mysterious ways'. At first I strongly resented the remark, especially the bit about becoming beggars, and thought her rude and cruel in the extreme. I even thought that she 'resented' our deliverance from the fate that she and others had envisioned for us. But when I thought about it later, after the initial anger had passed, I began to view the remark positively and tried to understand what she had said. Anyone who saw our circumstances during our childhood would agree with her that ours was a doomed family and believe that no human force on earth could reverse our fate. It is indeed true that it cannot be explained through ordinary human logic how we survived those initial years after our parents' death and the long years of struggle in our individual lives. In this sense this book is a testimony to God's infinite mercy and the generosity of the many kind souls who helped us on our way. Though many of our individual stories of survival are yet to be told, this book is a humble offering of Thanksgiving to God and all those who assisted us during the dark days of our childhood and adolescence.

Again, in certain other ways, I am also acting as a spokesperson for all my siblings who too have gone through the same hardships and dislocations and eventually prevailed. The material deprivations have long since been compensated, but it is the psychological scarring that may have left us wanting in many ways as adult siblings and even as parents. The past, which was our common heritage, remained long hidden in individual hearts. It is only now that much of that most painful period of our lives is laid bare here. The revelation is in a sense, an attempt at re-enforcing the core of our family which was so drastically altered for us when we were dispersed like so much chaff in the winds of misfortune. Two of my elder brothers and my only sister have passed on before reading a word of this book but they also had suffered and prevailed. That is why this book is dedicated to their memory too. But above all this book is an offering to the living who not only prevailed but also continue to cherish the present and are trying to build greater understanding and accommodation among, not only the survivors but more importantly among the next generation that has been so privileged when compared to our childhood circumstances.

This book is to a great extent, my confessional. I was dreaming of becoming someone and coming into my own. Instead, the end of High School found me in a totally baffling situation where some decisions were made for me which did not take into account what I wanted to do with my life. They were solely determined, once again by circumstances. I wanted to study further, more specifically to study medicine and become a doctor. But the general response to this fanciful wish was: 'who is going to pay for your studies?' Here I was then, stranded between my dreams and the stark reality of my situation which seemed insurmountable. Once again there was no 'home' for me to take shelter in; though both my elder brothers were married by then, their homes were not mine. One choice was to join my younger siblings in my uncle's home in the village. But then, what would I do there? It was as if I was a stray who needed to be rescued and tethered to a respectable post; and the obvious solution was that I had to be married off. At that point of time, the idea of marriage was remote and vague to me, it existed only in fairy-tale romances; it did not happen like this where barely a month out of boarding school you are virtually pushed into an alliance with a complete stranger and expected to become his shadow for the rest of your life. All my protestations were brushed aside and eventually I too gave in to the inevitable. My fate was sealed. For my family, the marriage was the best solution to the problem called Temsula, and they were overjoyed because they thought they found me the most perfect placement in life. But for me it was a mad plunge into the unknown. My predicament can be best compared to an un-initiated novice being pushed into a dark and alien space to contend with unfamiliar and dangerous players; my only weapons of self-defence being natural instincts and a will to survive.

The traumatic circumstances pertaining to our difficult childhood had remained locked away in my memory, and the fact that my memory retained these particular episodes out of many more perhaps, indicate that unbeknown to me they have had lasting influences on me during the formative years and have vicariously instilled a measure of toughness in my character. The story about our childhood, to my mind is the most important section and I needed to tell my loved ones what it was like to grow up with such a deep and constant longing for the remembered warmth of our parents' love and tender care, and always worrying from where our next meal would come. Children growing up without this vital sense of security can be compared to young saplings trying to cling to life in a desert.

Writing this has been cathartic in many ways. I have discovered that by facing the past, I have gained new strength to face the future. The ugly and the painful have become less so and now I can come out of the shell of self-isolation and even of shame sometimes about my miserable past by truthfully talking about a very difficult childhood and adolescence. It is not for nothing that we have this phrase, 'blessings in disguise'. Having known privation, indignity, hunger and deprivation of various kinds, I can relate more easily with the unfortunate ones of this world. In their circumstances I can recognise the travails of my own difficult past and that recognition has often prompted me to extend a helping hand or a kind word when I can do nothing more. I thank God that I am now in position to be of some help to such fellow beings. Perhaps by reaching out to them I am trying to rekindle in them too the resilience of the human spirit which helped me to overcome all these deprivations and has made me what I am today. In the process I have enlarged my circle of friends who constantly add to my emotional well-being. These are the blessings that have accrued to my life mainly because of all the earlier miseries.

I have travelled a long way since the time I realized that no matter how hard you thought about or longed for someone dead, s/he never comes back. Life has this forward-looking momentum that propels you to move ahead only. My life was such that most of the time I seemed to have no say in it and the best that I could do was to go along with these invisible and invincible forces. Articulating these often painful memories is my attempt to make sense of all that has happened to me so that I can understand myself better.

This story is mainly about my own life – as an ordinary woman who faced seemingly insurmountable odds from early childhood and who through sheer grit and self-belief overcame those vicissitudes of life. That I also happen to write a bit has added, I hope, a new perspective to the narrative.

And above all, I have written this book because I had to tell my story before time claimed it all.

Temsula Ao
Dimapur,
September 2011

PART I

Early Childhood

Recovering one's memories, I believe, is a sub-conscious process. Why it happens or when, is difficult to pinpoint. But it is a constant feature of one's life; for example we often find ourselves saying things like, 'when I was young' or 'when I was sick that year' often without realizing that these are all acts of this recovery process. Memories however are not one-to-one transferences; they emerge from multiple prisms of the subconscious of the 'rememberer'. The volition involved in the process to actually articulate these may vary from one person to another in terms of its semiotics, though the framework of presentation may remain the same. But the effort to do so in writing certainly requires a tremendous responsibility in terms of adhering to the true representation and relevance of the memories to one's life.

Writing about a childhood, which by any reckoning can be termed only as extremely difficult, becomes even more 'difficult' because impressions and actual memories of that phase of my life often come back to me as nebulous spectres in a lunar-like landscape dotted with blurred images; and again some as blocks of distinct events and experiences. There is no sequential ordering in these early memories and the kaleidoscopic recollections highlight only the defining moments of a childhood marred by early tragedy in the untimely death of the two most important persons in the life of any child, its parents.

Father

I begin with memories concerning my father, though it is not easy to recall his physical features or his voice. Whatever impressions I have of him have most probably been influenced by the few photographs of him and mother painstakingly restored by modern technology.

I see a young looking face, quite fair and broad with thick black hair. He is wearing a white shirt with half sleeves. It has an open collar. He is sitting with a woman on his right. Both look very self-conscious and serious. In another place he is standing with three other men; he is wearing very baggy shorts and there is a table in front of them with some dishes and tiny drinking goblets. The last one shows him lying on his back in a black-lined box; there are many flowers on and around him.

My father's name was Imnamathongba Changkiri and he was employed in the Christian Hospital at Borbhetta Mission Compound in Jorhat, Assam as Supervisor. We lived in a house within the big compound where the hospital was located, along with nurses' hostels and doctors' quarters, other staff quarters, a school and also a chapel attached to the hospital. Perhaps the earliest memories of this period are the times when father carried me on his shoulders when he went to the Sahib's bungalow to play badminton after work. I loved these outings because I got to sit on the lawns of the big two-storied house and watch my father and his friends, sometimes including the sahib, play noisy games. Father would not allow my elder brothers to accompany him saying that they had to finish their home-work. Seeing the big white man among the others made me wonder what kind of a 'man' he was.

There is another very distinct image in my mind which is most probably from this period where the sahib's entire family is depicted as though in a portrait.

It is a late afternoon scene and I see a bunch of horse riders circling our house on their way towards the other hospital beyond, where lepers were treated. Seated on what appeared to be enormous horses are the sahib, his beautiful wife, his two daughters and son. They are riding slowly and their golden hair is shining in the setting sun. It is an incredible scene. They don't look human at all. They look like some gods from another planet. I am suddenly very afraid and run and hide under the bed. Father is laughing at me, saying, 'Silly girl, why are you afraid? They are like us, only now they are on horses'. It was a rare sight because they normally kept to themselves and besides, the children were away in boarding school somewhere for most of the time.

(This was the family of Dr. O.W. Hasselblad, his wife Norma, their daughters Marva and Wyva and their son Carl out on their afternoon ride through the compound. This missionary couple was to play an important role in shaping my life when through their efforts, I was put in the boarding school at Golaghat.)

Though I did not realize it at that time, I was considered to be my father's favourite and therefore grew up as a pampered child. There were some reasons why everybody thought so, especially my brother Tajen. Father used to eat from a wooden plate carved out of a single piece of wood. It had four legs which gave the plate the required elevation as if it was placed on a low table. I loved those moments when he would call me at meal times and insist that I join him and many times mother would object by saying that I had already eaten. But father would have none of it and seating me by his side on a low stool, he would put choice morsels of meat tucked inside balls of rice in my mouth and watch me eat with pleasure. Such acts of 'favouritism' did not go un-noticed and were most resented by my brother Tajen and at every given opportunity he would either pinch me or pull my hair!

Though I did not observe anything different about father's treatment of me, later when I was growing up as an orphan, my uncle explained to me the reason for father's special affection for me. It appears that my parents lost two daughters older to my brothers and when I was born some years later my father was overjoyed. Then my younger brother was born and thus I was the only daughter among four children for quite some years.

Father seems to have had strict ideas about how to bring up children including his favourite. There are some incidents in my mind which clearly illustrate this. One evening I insisted on accompanying him to the sahib's bungalow; I had no idea why he was going there but I wanted to be with him. When we reached the bungalow, the sahib called him to his office and I followed. I saw that the white doctor had a pile of money on his table and after looking at a piece of paper he counted the money, stuffed it into a bag and handed the bag to my father. When he saw me, he called me over to where he was sitting and handed me a coin. It was heavy and white, not like the small ones I'd handled when mother was paying the vegetable man. This one was different and as I held it, I looked up at father. He was frowning and told me give it back. The sahib would not hear of it; he refused to take it back when I offered it to him. I looked up at father again and saw that he was still frowning so I put the coin on the table but the sahib said something to my father and put it back in my hand telling me to go out of the room. It was a most puzzling event; I did not understand why father did not want me to accept the money. I do not remember what happened to the coin; I only remember that it was the one and only time when I accompanied father on his monthly visits to the sahib's office to collect money to pay the employees of the compound the next day.

There was another incident which revealed father's

sterner side. One evening we, father, mother and me, visited a neighbour's house. While the grown-ups were busy chatting, my eyes fell on a cute little container on a side table. I surreptitiously opened the lid and saw that the lady had stored buttons of all colours and sizes in it. They looked so pretty! I immediately fell in love with that little golden-coloured container which appeared to have been made of a translucent material soft to the touch. I impulsively turned to the lady and asked, 'Aunty, can I have this?' Father nearly dropped his tea cup, and mother looked embarrassed. Before the lady could say anything, father said, 'No, you cannot have it.' But the hostess, without saying anything, picked up the container, emptied it and put in my hand. Father tried to snatch it from my hands to give it back. But I was adamant and clung to it saying, 'Aunty has given it to me.' When I began to whimper, my parents excused themselves and silently we walked home.

We reached home in silence and entered the front door which was quickly bolted by father.

I do not know what or who hit me but my right cheek is stinging and I hear father hiss in my ear, 'Go and return the case to aunty'. I must have done as he ordered because when I return still dreading father's reaction I find I am sitting on his lap and he is stroking my swollen cheek lovingly and saying to me, "You should never covet other people's things."

It was the first time when father was so stern with me and when I think of this incident sometimes, my cheek still smarts from the slap of a father who in spite of his love for a favourite child would not compromise on his principles. The trinket in question might have been insignificant, but the lesson he taught me has been invaluable.

There is a star-like scar on the inside of my left fore-arm which is the mark of an extraordinary boil that required surgery under anaesthesia. The actual events elude me; I only remember vaguely the evening when father carried me home in his arms the short distance from the hospital. I must have fallen asleep immediately because when I woke up, every one else, including my mother, had eaten dinner and were fast asleep. Only father had kept vigil over me. He helped me to the kitchen where he lit the fire to heat my dinner and served me. I started to eat with relish as he watched me. Suddenly there was an unearthly howling sound just outside the kitchen door and I was petrified, and went into a curling position, pushing the plate away. Father laughed and said, 'Don't worry, it's only a jackal. Do you want to see it?' At first I refused, but he insisted and emboldened by his urging, and staying close to him, we made for a chink in the bamboo wall of the kitchen, and there he was, a big dog-like creature sitting on his haunches and letting out those blood-curdling evil sounds. After watching him for a while, father shook the bamboo door and made threatening sounds with his mouth as well as stamping on the mud floor. As we watched, the jackal immediately slunk off towards the bushes nearby. This is one of the more frequent memories that I recall simply because whenever I think of the menacing jackal in my vicinity, I remember how unafraid I had become because father had his arms around me. I felt absolutely safe. There have been many instances in later life when I had often longed for the sense of security and well-being I felt when father was around.

The fact that I was considered father's favourite did not seem to matter much to the others. But as I have mentioned earlier, though my brother Tajen resented it, there was a time that he tried to take advantage of it. Father had a bicycle which he used for going to work and doing all other errands including going to the town market some three miles from home. It appears that there were strict instructions to my brothers never to touch it. But this brother of mine planned a stealthy ride for himself taking me with him as guarantee against father's anger. Accordingly one afternoon I was put on the pillion of the bicycle with strict instructions to hold my feet wide during the ride. But in the excitement, I forgot to do so and one of my heels was caught in the spokes slicing it neatly. When we came home, I was told later, the sliced heel was dangling by a thin strip of the sole and bleeding profusely. Father was home by that time and what happened next is also not exactly my recollection but has been gleaned from family lore.

After attending to my nearly severed heel in the hospital, father brought me home and went straight for his bamboo cane. It is said that he shattered the cane on my brother and curiously, he himself was weeping, perhaps from extreme anger or fear that worse could have happened, not only to me but to both of us because my brother had not yet learnt how to ride a bicycle properly. It was only after this incident, I was told that father allowed my brothers to learn cycling under his supervision.

I remember certain scenes from our visit to our ancestral village during the winter season. Father insisted on taking the children to the village whenever possible to meet our assorted uncles, aunts, cousins and older relatives. (Later on I was told that father did this so that we who were born and brought up in the plains would not forget our roots.) Only a few incidents have remained in my memory of such visits. One is of a white-haired lady placing a freshly laid egg in my palm and saying, 'Tell your mother to boil it for you'. She, I was told later, was my father's paternal aunt who had practically brought him up after his mother was struck by a debilitating disease and did not survive long. This grand-aunt absolutely doted on father and every time he came to the village, I was told, hers would be the first house he visited.

There is another story about this grand-aunt. Initially

when father took up the job in Jorhat, he left mother with our two elder brothers in the village. It took some years before he could make arrangements for them to come and live with him there. Since she was so close to my father, our brothers visited her house very frequently and during these visits, she used to give them home-brewed rice beer. My eldest brother used to say how much he enjoyed that heady brew! Incidentally, all Naga households in those days brewed their own rice beer which was consumed as part of the regular meals. Only after they converted to Christianity, they were made to abandon this practice because it was considered to be heathen. But for my brothers it was a real treat because mother's family embraced the new religion quite early and mother obviously frowned on it. For a long time it seems mother did not know about my brothers drinking rice beer in grand-aunt's house because just before going home, she would make them chew raw ginger to remove the smell from their mouths! I still remember how my eldest brother enjoyed recounting this childhood tale whenever we discussed those visits to the village. Mother herself had never touched the stuff and when eventually she discovered why her sons clamoured to go to the old lady's house so frequently, she used to make them open their mouths on their return to test whether they had drunk the brew again!

Another unique memory regarding those visits is of my great fear of venturing on to the bamboo platform at the back of every house which was used as a back veranda. I could see the earth below it through the chinks and I was scared that I would fall through if I stepped on it! For a small child perhaps these were some exciting and exotic experiences. But now I can see how these visits indeed helped us to maintain close relationships with our relatives in the village all through our growing-up. I also realize why father wanted us to be aware of who we were and why we should never forget our roots. When I view contemporary society today and see the growing alienation of our urban population from their own 'folk' in the villages, I can truly appreciate my father's vision and his attempts at forging this all-important bond that has given us a strong sense of belonging to our ancestral village. It also helped my siblings when they were sent to the village to live there after our parents' death because they did not feel that they were among strangers; in fact they adapted to the new environment without any difficulty.

The one vivid memory of father I have is of the time when he was taken to the hospital on a stretcher one evening. It seems I had measles and I was in bed. Father complained of a severe toothache during his lunch break and could not eat anything and went straight to bed. By evening it had become so bad that he had to be taken on a stretcher to the hospital though it was only a short distance from our house. Though all these details came to me later, the scene where I am standing on the bed and telling him, 'Father come home soon' and the look he gave me is still imprinted on my mind. That was the last time I saw father alive.

That night I woke up from a feverish sleep and what I saw has been one of the most vivid memories of my childhood and is as fresh in my mind as if it happened only the other night. All the lights were on in the room where I usually slept with my parents in a big bed. Mother was sitting up with my youngest brother at her breasts; her long black hair was hanging loose, her upper body was completely bare, tears dripping from her eyes she was gazing out of the wide open window into the darkness beyond. She did not notice that I was awake and that my brother was whimpering because the teat was out of his mouth. She sat immobile, oblivious of her surrounding and seemed so far away. It was only much later, when I grew up and used to think about this

midnight scene that I began to comprehend the enormity of
her bereavement. Father was away from home only a few
hours when the news must have been broken to her. The
suddenness of it and the sheer improbability of it all: they
said he bled to death after a tooth was extracted. As a child,
nothing of this registered or perhaps even mattered. But as
I grew older and was able to think, I began to wonder how
could such a catastrophe have happened to him on account
of a mere tooth? And how this set in motion the process of
mother's early death and the eventual disintegration of our
family. I still wonder.

People said that mother was calm during the funeral
service; she even sang a farewell song for my father from
the Ao hymn book. My aunts remembered the number and
told me later. It is a hymn which talks about heaven and
speculates what it must be like up there. Perhaps it was
mother's belief that she would meet him there one day. What
a staunch believer, they said; what a model wife and mother.
They also said that she was a strong person and would be
able to look after the family somehow. She certainly must
have given the spectators that impression about herself. But
only as an adult did I realize that it was her public persona
and no one could have really understood the depth of her
sorrow at losing the mainstay and anchor of her being, of
being stranded with six children in a home not her own and
away from her own people, barely literate and not fit for
any employment. It must have been the enormity of this
incalculable bereavement that had such an impact on her
will and led her to an early grave.

There is a large family photograph of father's funeral
which shows him lying inside a black-lined coffin, a bouquet
of white flowers and green leaves on the white sheet covering
him up to his chest, and a profusion of flowers covering
the coffin lid. Mother is wearing a white sari with a border

holding my youngest brother and gazing intently at father. She looks so young and forlorn. It shows me with puffed eyes, dishevelled hair, wearing a crumpled frock standing among my siblings and assorted cousins, uncles and aunts, all facing the open coffin.

Mother

My mother's name was Nokyintemla Longkumer. As with father's, my memory of mother's physical appearance is also reconstructed mostly from photographs.

I see a woman sitting next to a serious-looking man. She is wearing what appears to be a sari because it seems as though a pallu is flung over her left shoulder. She is broad-faced and seems to be much fairer than the man. Her hair is black and seems to be loose. She is wearing an old-fashioned blouse with a lace-trimmed collar and short puffed sleeves. Again in another place she is standing with a group of men and women where father is also present. And I am somewhat shocked to see that she seems to be taller than father. Then she is sitting on a chair behind a sewing machine as if she is stitching something.

Family lore has it that the sewing machine in question was bought from American soldiers when they were leaving their station in Jorhat after the end of World War II. We have been told that father bought some pieces of furniture including the sewing machine for which alone he paid Rs.10. Both of them were immensely proud of this possession, especially mother. And why not? After all, for a not so average middle-class family to own an American sewing machine was no mean achievement! Never mind if it was only a second-hand one, mother could turn out many shirts and frocks for her children. Sometimes neighbours also came and wanted to sew their clothes on it. But they had to do it in our house because it was a foot machine and not easily transportable.

But more importantly, mother would never agree to let it out of her sight!

I mention this because this machine is now in my possession. After I got married, my paternal uncle one day took me aside and said,' There are only two things which you and your younger sister can claim as your inheritance from your parents; one is a pair of gold earrings and the other is the sewing machine. Since you are older, you have the first choice, what do you say?' Without a moment's hesitation I chose the machine which is my proudest possession and is in excellent condition even today after more than half a century since it came to our family. I sometimes wonder how old the machine must be: it does look old and has the number 22 embossed on its Singer frame. But it is sturdy and can run through even the toughest material like denim. Though as females, my sister and I could have no share of father's landed property in the village, I am content with this token of inheritance which constantly reminds me of who I am and where I came from.

It may sound ludicrous to talk about an ancient sewing machine as a piece of valuable 'inheritance' but for me this machine is precious and is the only tangible evidence that my parents lived on this earth too. It is my only link to them in a material sense. I am sure that my sister also has the same feelings about the chunky and somewhat old-fashioned pair of gold earrings that adorned mother and are now in her possession.

I need to elaborate a little more about my reaction on seeing the old machine in a small room of my uncle's house after my marriage. I was shocked and at the same time ashamed to realize that in the intervening years of growing up, away from immediate family contacts while I was in the boarding school, the memory of my parents had begun to fade and grow distant. When uncle showed me the piece of my 'inheritance', it was like a jolt from the past and I was reminded of the fact that I did have a mother and father once upon a time and this was the humble legacy that they had left behind for me. In a very curious way I felt that an old link was restored; and since that moment the machine has become a symbol of that reconnection rather than a mere material possession.

The death of a loved one diminishes the survivors in many different ways. When father died so suddenly, mother must have felt that her life was over. When she too died just nine months after father's death, the villagers began to talk about their love and devotion to each other in almost legendary terms. They said that true lovers like them never live long together. They even used to cite examples from folklore to illustrate that true lovers either never find fulfilment in marriage, and even if they do, they never get to spend old age together. Such talk may perhaps be dismissed as ignorant superstition of rural folk but there are ample examples of ill-fated lovers in many other cultures too. And the fact remains that mother did not survive long after father's death. The only difference here is that while the other stories are romantic examples from folklore and legends, my parents' case shows that such tragedies are played out in the lives of ordinary mortals too.

It must have been extremely difficult for mother to carry the burden of the family with not enough material and psychological support. My eldest brother was taken in to do a part of the job that father was did, which meant that he must have been paid only a fraction of what father was paid. Mother tried to give us the best she could but with the seeming cruelty of children born out of ignorance about the realities of the adult world, we could not accept the changes in our life-style, especially me. The first instance was my birthday which I expected to be as before when father was

alive. There would be a new frock, new shoes and lots of
goodies to share with friends. But all that mother could afford
on that day were some cookies she made with our initials on
them. As an adult and a mother, I now know how much it
hurt her when I refused to eat them.

And then, there was the first Christmas without father.
Every year, it was during this time that we all got new
clothes and new shoes. How I loved to wear the new shoes to
Christmas service, exaggerating every step so that the crepe
soles squeaked loudly! But there would be no new shoes this
year, mother announced. In that case, I replied I will not
wear old shoes on Christmas morning. As you please, mother
must have said. And sure enough on Christmas morning I
walked with the family to church barefoot. When mother
saw me, she stood still, a stricken look on her face. But I
was stubborn and refused to listen to her. She said I would
catch a cold if I walked barefoot on such a cold morning. But
I would not give in and walked on. It was only when I sat
down on the bench that the winter cold on my soles began
to creep up my legs and gripped me in such a way that I
could barely sit straight. It was the most agonizing hour of
my life and I don't remember whether I cried afterwards
or said anything to my mother. But even as write this, I am
overwhelmed by an immense sorrow and infinite regret for
causing my mother so much grief over a pair of shoes and
wish that I had a chance to say how sorry I am for inflicting
this cruelty on her. Now that I am a mother myself and have
gone through many agonizing moments for not being able to
give all the things that the children demanded, I realize how
much mother must have suffered that Christmas morning
for not being able to match her love with material gifts.

Though there were other forms of deprivations, we
appear to have had a regular life after father's death for
sometime mainly due to mother's marshalling the meagre

family resources. We never went hungry when she was alive. The regular routines of going to school and church continued. What I remember about mother was her regular attendance in the Women's Services in the compound held in various households on certain days of the week. On those days mother always wore a sari or the Assamese 'mekhela sador'. After she died, it seems that her saris and mekhela sadors were taken to the village to be kept for me and my sister. But by the time I was ready to wear them, the numbers had dwindled and what remained had grown old and worn out as a result of my aunts' experimenting with them in the village!

Some other incidents come to mind about my 'tussles' with mother. I loved to eat raw tomatoes but mother forbade it because I would deplete her kitchen resources. But several times I would sneak into the kitchen when I thought mother was elsewhere, pick the ripest and biggest of the lot, take it behind the kitchen and eat it ravenously. Though mother it seems did know about it, she never said anything. I realized it only when the small-pox vaccination, so painfully jabbed on my left arm in the shape of an isosceles triangle festered and gave me much discomfort for quite sometime. During dinner one evening, she told my brothers who also had the same shots but did not seem to have any problems, 'These wounds always fester when one eats raw fruits or vegetables, especially tomatoes'. When she said that I began to wonder why she never reprimanded me; now I think that perhaps she thought ripe tomatoes were a small compensation for all the other things she could not provide us. The sores eventually healed but I still bear the prominent scars on my left arm and the memory of my silent embarrassment.

Another incident about mother's stoic acceptance of things relates to my brother Tajen. The year that my father died, he failed in the final exams. Mother had heard about it from the Headmaster of the school who also lived in the compound. But she waited for my brother to bring home the report card. When he came home, mother was washing clothes in the public tap near our house. She saw him coming but did not say anything, just continued with her washing. My brother went to the kitchen, ate something and then only he came out and walked up to my mother holding the report card. Without looking up mother asked, 'What happened? Have you passed?' He simply extended the hand holding the report card for her to read. She looked up at him and began to mumble, she was on the verge of tears. Though she already knew that he had failed, seeing the word on the card must have broken her resolve not to show her grief and disappointment. After some time she wiped her eyes and began to scold him, 'You are no good, you are headstrong, disobedient and now this. I do not know what will become of you'. By now she was really crying hard. Seeing her so distraught, my brother burst out, 'Ok if I am no good, I'll go and lay myself on the railway track and then you will be happy'. So saying he began to walk away but turned once again and said, 'Mother I am going to commit suicide'. She lost all patience then and shouted, 'Ok, go and do it, I don't care!'

He was gone for a long time, and mother went around the house listlessly as if she was not there at all. I had forgotten all about the shouting match and was playing with my friends in the courtyard when I spotted my brother coming towards the house. It was getting on to be evening and I could not make out what he was holding in his hand. Coming closer, he shouted to me, 'See what I got for you'. It was a small fish strung on a reed, still wriggling and I noticed that he was covered in mud from head to foot! He never reached the railway tracks; but had spent the whole day wading in the muddy waters of the nearby stream! He had perhaps thought that by bringing in the peace offering to me, mother would once again accept him as he was: naughty, disobedient and still failed. I do not remember what happened to the fish and how mother reacted to his return, but she soon became her own stoic self, trying to do her best in an extremely difficult situation. But even today when I see a fish dangling from the end of a string or reed, I remember my brother's tentative approach and his muddied clothes and realise that he too must have felt the immense void in our lives after father's death and was struggling to cope with the loss. It becomes apparent only now that we reacted in our different ways to the tragedy and our behaviour must have reflected our sense of bewilderment at the sudden and unexpected turn in our lives.

Although, I do not have any clear image of my mother's physical appearance except that provided by photographs, there is a very distinct image in my mind of a naked woman who happened to be my mother. It is not so much about individual aspects of that being but of the notion of nudity which one finds difficult to associate with one's own mother. This was quite different from the night of my father's death when I saw her naked torso but this did not disturb me so much because I was accustomed to seeing her breasts when she suckled my youngest brother.

This momentous incident when I saw mother naked happened in the daytime. We did not have an attached bathroom like many people do nowadays. This facility was away from the main house, screened off by bamboo matting. One day I heard mother calling out to me from the bathroom. When I went near, she asked me to bring her towel which she had forgotten to take with her. I went to the house to fetch it and went near the bathroom to give it to her. I stood outside the door and called out. She could have stretched her hand and taken it from me but she asked me to come inside.

I did so unsuspectingly; but what I saw when I entered the bathroom riveted me to the spot. She was squatting on a low stool completely naked and without even glancing at me, asked me to hang the towel on the nail put there for the purpose as she continued pouring water on herself. My first reaction was one of bewilderment and even shock maybe. The fact that mother was not at all ashamed to be naked before me was puzzling. After hanging up the towel I came out hurriedly without saying a word.

But the image of the woman I just saw inside the bathroom baffled me immensely: was she really my mother? What I saw inside was a person who was very fair, had enormous breasts, her wet hair covered parts of her body, and in the squatting position, her thighs protruded below the stomach in a manner that hid her genitals from view. This woman looked so different from the image of mother in a sador-mekhela, with hair neatly combed and tied into a bun and ready with Bible and Hymn Book to go to Sunday service. I found it difficult to reconcile the naked woman in the bathroom with the sedately dressed one in public. From an early age girls are taught about the 'shame' of nudity and are always cautioned to be 'careful'. Then why did mother not feel any 'shame' in letting me see her like this? I shall never know but recalling this incident, a question often comes to my mind; does nudity reveal or hide one's true identity?

We used to get occasional visitors from the village, mainly relatives who stayed with us. They came either to purchase essential commodities like salt and kerosene or had some medical problems to be attended to in the hospital. Among such visitors there was once a woman who smoked a pipe filled with tobacco grown in her garden in the village. The pipe was made of some kind of tin and had a bamboo nozzle through which she smoked. The moment I saw the pipe I was taken up by curiosity and looked for an opportunity to steal a few draws on the lit pipe. Very soon the opportunity presented itself: one day the woman had just lit the pipe and was beginning to draw on it when she was called out of the house by someone. She put the pipe on a stool and rushed out. Seeing this as the chance I was looking for, I grabbed hold of the pipe and took a mighty drag which nearly choked me. Something nasty hit my chest and I dropped the pipe and barely made it to our room where I collapsed on the bed. They told me later that I slept the whole day and well into the night as a result of my experiment with the deadly pastime of village women. I do not remember if mother said anything to me but they all knew what caused my sudden collapse and long slumber.

Another time there was a 'tussle' with my mother when she stitched a new frock for me on her machine. I refused to wear it because it did not have a pocket in the front as on the others I had. Mother said that since I had so many frocks which had pockets, I could try wearing this one without a pocket for a change and tried to divert my attention, 'See, how nice and soft the cloth is and the flowers look so pretty. I have also added some ribbons at the waist. It will look better without the pockets.' I did not say anything but secretly resolved to add the pocket myself. I liked to watch mother when she sat on her sewing machine and operated the pedals to stitch clothes for us as well as other utility items for the kitchen. So I thought I knew how to handle the machine. One day when mother was out, I took a piece of the cloth out of which the new frock was made and inserting the frock first under the needle, placed the piece meant to be a pocket at what I thought to be the right place. I tried to start the machine but it stalled. I stepped hard on the treadle and the result was a big snarl of thread and cloth below the needle. I was terrified and tried to pull out the whole thing and in doing so broke the needle and caused a big tear in the new frock. What happened afterwards, I cannot exactly recall. But I am sure that I never wore that contentious frock. And after this incident, it would take me a long time to be able to wear a new frock because just nine months after father's death, mother also died.

Much of what happened to mother and how she died is gleaned from the accounts given by relatives. It seems that for a while she did try to be strong and brave for the sake of the family. But not for long. When the enormity of her loss began to sink in, they say she began to lose all interest in life without father. She became listless and began to lose weight. She even missed many Women's Services. She languished for a few months and when she finally went to the doctor, he told her that she had have an operation to remove a growth inside her. At least this is the version given to us. She was admitted into the hospital and operated upon. While recuperating from the surgery, they say she caught a cold and began to cough and as a result of which some of the stitches split open. The wound festered and became sceptic. There was no drug at that time to arrest the infection and within a few days she died.

What I vaguely remember about this incident is that we, I and my younger brother, went to visit mother in the hospital. She was in a room by herself and we thought that she was asleep. But when we entered she opened her eyes, turned to us and gave a faint smile but after that she turned her face to the wall. We stood there for sometime, my brother and I wondering what to do. We called out to her but she did not respond. A nurse came in after some time and gently led us outside telling us to go home. It was the last time I saw mother, her face turned away from us. To this day this scene haunts me; was mother unhappy with us? Was it because of the pathetic bouquet of wild flowers I was holding? Or was she already grieving for us because she knew that she was going to die and leave us alone and helpless? Why did she turn her face away from us? I will never know the answer. But that does not in any way lessen the sense of grief and even of rejection that tugs at my heart, even as I am writing this. And at every recall, I find myself asking, why, mother, why?

It so happened that mother died early on an Easter Sunday and because her funeral was to be held that afternoon, the regular morning Easter Service was postponed to the evening. We, the Sunday School students had been practicing a song to be sung on Easter service long before mother was taken to the hospital. That she had died that morning does not seem to have made any impact on our minds. Nor do I recall anything like grief or sadness about that particular day. I do not remember how we spent the day, or where the funeral was. It appears that everything about that day has been blocked out of my consciousness. The only recollection I have of it is the song that we had to sing in church. So we went to the evening service to sing a special number. Guided by the teacher we were assembled at the doorstep of the chapel, standing in two rows, each of us given an Easter lily in full bloom and were instructed to sing as we entered the chapel. We were to walk slowly, singing all the while and when we reached the pulpit, were to place the flowers in the two vases kept on each side of the pulpit. As rehearsed, we entered, holding a lily each, and singing. For the children, including my brother and I, it was just another service where we were performing. The heart-breaking pathos of our participation in this song was recognized by the adults and later we were told that when the congregation saw me and my brother marching with the group, they cried seeing us orphans joining in the celebration of Christ's resurrection so soon after our own mother was put in her grave.

Could anyone be held responsible for the display of insensitivity connected with our participation in the singing

of the special number? Should the teachers have kept us out
of it? I shall never know. But I have always had an ambivalent
attitude to Easter Sunday since then, no matter on what date
this important event in the Christian calendar falls every
year. Young though I was, my subconscious must have
registered something negative about that particular day. This
day is supposed to be a day of celebration, a day of triumph
for all believers; in fact the core of the Christian faith rests
on the Resurrection of Christ. But for me, that Easter Sunday
was a day when I intuitively felt that something awful had
happened to us. And as I grew older and understood the full
implication of the event, the day seems to have been divested
of its religious significance, though I profess to be a Christian.
Instead, it has acquired a negative symbolism as a day of great
personal loss. Easter Sundays may not coincide with the date
when mother died but the association of the two events still
troubles me and I cannot help feeling depressed on the day
which is supposed to be a day of rejoicing for all believers.

Though mother's actual death and funeral did not leave
any palpable memory in my mind, the fact that she was not
there began to affect me gradually. I always expected to hear
her voice when I came home from school, expected to hear
her say, 'Go wash your hands' or 'change your frock' when
I came back from playing with my friends. Instead, there
would be this eerie silence in a cold kitchen. The rest of the
house also seemed strange without her presence. I began
to brood alone. I no longer enjoyed running and screaming
with my friends. I sought the company of other mothers in
the compound, listening to their conversations and wishing
for mother to be with them. Seeing the other mothers always
made me jealous of their children. But I continued stalking
these mothers wherever I saw them. One day while I was
passing by the public tap, two of these women were talking.
What they were saying stopped me in my tracks: they

were talking about mother. One said that she saw mother drawing water from the tap the previous evening; but when she called out, mother simply turned her back and took the road towards the cemetery. The other replied that she must have been thinking too much about her, that is why mother showed herself to her and warned her not to do so anymore. When the women saw me, they just gave me a funny look and walked away.

I began to think about what the second woman said: if you think hard enough about a dead person, you can actually see her! So I tried to recollect mother's face, her voice and even the clop-clop sound she made when she walked in her wooden sandals, all in the hope that sooner or later mother would show herself to me. It became an obsession with me: mother must show herself to me because I was thinking of her all the time. During this period I used to wake up early and listen intently for sounds coming out of the kitchen. When mother was alive, it was always she who woke up first and made her clop-clop way towards the kitchen to light the fire. She would use the bamboo cylinder to blow on the charcoal to get the fire going. After she made the tea, she would call out to us to come and get it. There were many mornings when I imagined that I heard all these sounds from the kitchen. Then I would tip-toe barefoot to the kitchen intending to surprise her with a big boo! But each time I eased the door open with this expectation, only the cold ashes of the fireplace greeted me with their deadness. At every such disappointment, the loneliness in my heart would intensify. But I was adamant: mother must show herself to me because I was thinking of her all the time. As time went on, this daily ritual of listening to sounds I expected to hear heralding mother's presence in the kitchen and the ultimate dejection of not finding her there became an intolerable burden in my heart.

I could not talk about this to anyone; my younger brother would not understand. And I could certainly not approach my elder brothers; I was always a bit afraid of them because of the difference in our ages and tried to keep aloof from them. So I simply suffered and languished with the burden of my unspeakable longing and grief. But I continued with the early morning ritual of listening for sounds of mother's presence in the kitchen, imagining that I heard them. But every morning the result would be the same: there would be no mother in the empty kitchen. I did not want to give up my attempt to bring mother back by thinking of her as hard as I could. But however hard I tried, I could not sustain the pretence for much longer and had to accept the fact that mother was never going to come back to us. That was the day that a part of me died.

Perhaps this was the moment which is described by Maya Angelou as 'being aware of (her) displacement' of the protagonist in *I Know Why the Caged Bird Sings*. In my case it was not so much a sense of 'displacement' yet but of total 'abandonment'. My life seems to have taken a definitive turn with the knowledge that mother was never going to come back or even show herself to me, no matter how 'hard' I thought about her and longed for her to come back. The finality of this knowledge totally devastated me. While I felt utterly lonely, I also felt terribly let down and betrayed, but in the ignorance of childhood I could not determine by whom or what. It was then that I think that the blissfully ignorant little girl with a stalk of lily walking up the aisle that Easter evening stepped into a world of palpable pain and deprivation with no reprieve in sight. The impact of this awareness was a debilitating malady of the mind that began to take its toll on my body too.

Some kindly nurses who were my mother's friends and who regularly visited our house must have noticed the change in me: I had lost weight, was listless and became deathly pale. They decided I needed some tonic and procured it for me in the form of cod-liver oil, ten drops of which had to be consumed in a glass of milk every day. I hated the stuff; the first few times they forced me to drink the horrid concoction, I threw up. They then began counselling me saying how good it was for me, that I would grow stronger, could go to school regularly and play with my friends. They showed me how to compress my nose with my fingers while I poured the polluted milk down my throat. It was not so bad, this method of swallowing the foul-smelling remedy. Under the surveillance of these Good Samaritans, I managed to keep down the tonic and after some time I convinced them that I could manage without their supervision. They reluctantly agreed and I began to play a trick. Into the milk would go five drops of the terrible oil and the other five would be squirted out of the window. And on certain days I would simply squirt all ten drops into the ground outside the window and drink the milk only. But one day a nurse caught me in the act and my ordeal continued for quite sometime more under their strict supervision. Whether this helped me in any way, I cannot say for sure. But what I can say with absolute certainty is that I HATE cod-liver oil to this day!

The process of sifting through the memories of my past life obviously entailed making a conscious decision about which ones to record and which to reject. There was a particular incident in the village when father died, and I had wanted it to remain just another bit of very painful memory. I had set it aside because I felt that I would not be comfortable writing about it even after so many years. But when I read what I had written about my parents, I was struck by a sense that somehow my narrative had not fully captured the essence of their life spent in this land, 'not their own' and that it merely chronicled their sojourn like that of any displaced migrant family. I instantly realized that the portrayal was incomplete because as I matured and interacted with so many relatives as well as complete strangers who had known father, I was convinced that there was more to father's life than my sketchy account of what happened during their 'temporary' sojourn in Jorhat. I decided to include this particular incident also because the sequel to the incident was played out in our house shortly after father's death. And in order to do that, it is necessary to give a brief historical context to father's life before his Jorhat sojourn and death.

Father belonged to a founding clan of our village Changki and from his youth was acknowledged as a born leader. However he could study only up to class VIII in the Jorhat Mission High School after which he successfully completed a typing training course. It is said that for some time he even worked as a government vaccinator in the Health Department, a job which saw him travel far and wide to many remote villages in the then Naga Hills District of Assam. By and by he got married and became the proud father of two sons, my elder brothers Kharibong and Tajenyuba. But the seemingly peaceful life in the village was soon to be disrupted by circumstances way beyond his control.

Father's clan and particularly father was always the target for his rivals, a clan which was constantly manoeuvring to distort village history and establish their superiority in the village hierarchy. Unfortunately for father, his rivals had powerful allies in the British administration in the head office in Mokokchung and they took advantage of the fact. While studying in Jorhat, father and a friend of his was accused of attending a political rally there and his rivals began circulating false rumours about his activities. He was portrayed as a supporter of Gandhi and his travels on duty were construed as campaigns to turn innocent villagers against the British. Though nothing substantial could be proved against father, his rivals managed to have him expelled from the village for a certain period of time. Fearing that he might be physically assaulted by his rivals, his supporters advised father to leave the village under cover of darkness. But father refused, saying that he was not a thief that he should flee his birthplace stealthily. He said he would depart at daybreak to honour the village decree but promised he would be back soon. Elderly people in the village still remember the song that father sang as he went out of the village with just the clothes on his back. He came to Jorhat because it was the only familiar place where he had lived for a number of years during his high school days.

Before he found any a job, he fell ill and needed to have an emergency surgery. But he had no money to pay for the operation, so father struck a deal with the doctor. He requested the doctor to operate on him and promised that after he recovered, he would stay on and do any menial job the doctor demanded of him without wages and thus pay off his debt. The doctor agreed and soon enough, father recovered and started doing all kinds of odd jobs around the compound until he paid off his debt to the hospital. When the doctor saw how sincere and hardworking father was, he offered him a regular job as soon as the cost of surgery was paid off. Thereafter father brought mother and my two elder brothers from the village and their new life began in the Jorhat Mission Hospital. This is also how the four younger children were born in Jorhat Mission Hospital; me, my brother Jangtsulong, my sister Sutsungkala and my youngest brother Achemtsungba.

Over the years, as I introspected on their new life and more specifically came to learn about father's dealings with both his boss and other employees, I had become convinced of one fact: that father was a man who was never shaken from his belief in himself. Though he was so totally

dependant on the white sahib for the survival of his family,
father never compromised on his principles. Among the
many stories about father who had now become Supervisor
of the establishment, there is one which illustrates this
point. It seems that father once went to the loft where the
hospital linen was dried during rainy days and through a
chink in the floor, he saw the doctor smoking in his chamber
down below. He was shocked that the boss was indulging in
something which was strictly prohibited among the other
employees. He had also heard whispers about some other
indiscretions about the doctor's dealings with some of the
employees. Taking the smoking incident as an excuse,
father barged into the chamber and confronted his boss and
warned him to be more careful. The doctor simply could not
believe that a subordinate could confront him like that and
he became incensed by this open attack. They had a fierce
altercation which ended with father flinging the bunch of
keys in his custody at the angry doctor declaring that he
was quitting the job. That day he came home before lunch
time and told mother what had happened. They must have
thought that they would be going back to the village. But
they were in for a surprise; the doctor came to the house
in the evening! It must have hurt his ego acutely but the
chastised doctor swallowed his pride and begged father to
stay on, saying that he and the hospital needed him. He
also promised that he would behave correctly in the future!
Father relented and this incident marked the turning point
in the equation between them because it is said that from
that time on, father became not a mere employee but a good
friend and confidante of the doctor.

This change in father's status in the eyes of his boss was
to have far-reaching consequences for our family. When
he died so suddenly, the doctor immediately inducted
my eldest brother into father's post, though in a part-time

capacity. He allowed the family to stay on in the company house for as long as it was necessary. And above all, it was through the intervention of this missionary couple that I was admitted in the boarding school at Golaghat where, I believe, the expenses were mainly borne by them. In reality, it was their benevolence which gave me the opportunity to have an excellent education which became the corner-stone of my subsequent academic achievements.

But back to the incident I alluded to earlier; and to present it in the right perspective, it is necessary to refer back to the historical context beginning with father's exodus to Jorhat as the unfortunate victim of village rivalry. As I reflect on this aspect of his life in the 'alien' land, I have gained an insight that is relevant to all: to every life lived on this earth, there is an inner context, the context of a person's birth and heritage, no matter how obscure or insignificant it may seem to an outsider. He is both a product of and subject to this truth. The person's life is lived out, be it in his own environment or an alien one, like that of my father's, with this intrinsic context, and the worth of that life is eventually measured in terms of the person's integrity to the context. My father never wavered from his existential context because of which, even if he was leading the life of an 'exile' as it were, he was still a strong moral force to reckon with in the village polity. His rivals, recognizing this fact, were constantly afraid of him. They might have succeeded in removing his physical presence from the village for a time but the shadow of Mathong seems to have persistently haunted his rivals. And after the ban period was over, father used to make regular visits to the village with us children because he wanted us too, to stay in touch with our roots. With every visit of father's, their paranoia increased and that is why when they heard of his sudden death, they considered it as some kind of victory for them and reacted in a most uncivilized way.

According to eyewitnesses, both relatives and other villagers, when the news of my father's death reached the village, his rivals gathered in the house of the leader and celebrated the event publicly, jumping up and down with joy and shouting over and over again, 'Can Mathong really die?' Not only that, they also sent bursts from shotguns into the air to emphasize their sense of triumph at father's demise. When mother heard of it later from visiting relatives, she did not say anything but only wept in her room. But with my two elder brothers, it was different. Their young blood boiled and they vowed vengeance on these people who could celebrate the death of father in such a cruel and humiliating way. Our relatives in the village who saw this open display of hatred for father and all that he stood for, never tired of talking about this whenever batches of them visited our home after his death. It became the most painful blow to mother's grieving heart and for my brothers, an unspeakable burden they carried all their lives.

But mother kept her sorrows to herself and continued the routine that she had followed when father was alive. Visiting the hospital in the afternoons was a part of that routine. She kept it up even after his death; it must have helped her to forget her own sorrows temporarily by comforting the sick and perhaps by continuing with her old routine, she was also trying to restore some semblance of normalcy to her life. Not very long after father's death, news came that the leader of father's rival group was admitted to the Jorhat hospital with a serious condition. They said that the problem was in the intestines and an incision had to be made on the stomach so that the body waste from the system could be evacuated through a pipe inserted through the opening. It was also said that the odour from the drainage was such that even the nurses were reluctant to go near his bed in the general ward.

When my brothers heard of it, they warned mother not to go near him during her daily visits to the hospital. But in spite of their warning, mother did visit him; stench and all, whether out of curiosity or some other compelling reason, no one can say. When my brothers heard about mother's visit, they were furious and said many bitter and angry things. She simply listened to them and is reported to have said, 'I am simply visiting a sick man from our own village who has no relatives to speak of beside his bed. God sees all and He will judge accordingly'. She not only visited him, she even coerced my brother Tajen to carry food for the sick man twice. The second time when she asked him, he flatly refused by saying that he could not go near the bed because he stank so badly. However he later confessed to a nephew that ultimately he had to go because mother threatened to cane him! The sick man did not survive long in this condition and died soon after. Like father he also had to be buried in Jorhat, for taking a body back to the village was out of the question in those days because there was no motorable road to our village. It appears that two of his sons arrived only the next morning and they were desperate to find a place to prepare the coffin and serve at least a cup of tea to the few attendants and mourners, mostly some local Christians and some Nagas from the Police Reserve.

It is at this point that the final act in the rivalry between father and this man was played out on the latter's funeral day. When the sons came to arrange it, they found themselves in a totally strange environment where they knew no one except our family. Since mother was the only person they could talk to, they came to her asking her permission to stop at our house. They also wanted to borrow a big dekchi to brew tea in our kitchen! When my brothers heard about this, they were outraged and fumed: 'How dare they?' They demanded that mother deny them permission; but mother was not going to listen to them. She only told the helpers to put a paste of mud on the outside of the big vessel so that it would not become blackened by the wood fire and she also stipulated that they clean it themselves afterwards. My brothers however were furious; they stomped out of the house to show their disgust at mother's action and stayed out until the funeral party proceeded towards the same cemetery where father had been buried only a few months earlier. Thus the few arrangements for the funeral of the man who had rejoiced at father's death had to be carried out in the home of the man whom they had vilified in life and did not spare in death either.

There is a saying among the rural folk that the dying day truly proves the real worth of a person. All his life, father had been the object of his rivals' vilification but on his last ride, this leader of the rival gang had to stop over at the house of the same man at whose death, he and his pals had so recently expended celebratory bullets into the skies. As I write about this bizarre incident, I begin to wonder if this very awkward and humiliating situation faced by his sons was an abject lesson to a people, who in the past had lived with the honour code that even the body of a slain enemy had to be treated with respect. Death is the moment signalling the cessation of hostilities and in the old days, anyone coming across a dead body in the jungle, be it friend or foe, was morally bound to transport it to the deceased's family. Failure to do so would result in severe stricture from the village authorities and there would be the inevitable fine. But rejoicing at anyone's death even that of an enemy's, and that too so publicly, was unheard of and constituted a blatant violation of this time-honoured community code of respect for the dead.

I cannot say if mother was thinking of that painful moment when she first heard of the celebration at father's death when she allowed her biggest aluminium dekchi pasted with mud to be used for brewing tea for the funeral of her husband's most bitter rival. To my mind, it was supremely ironic because it must have been galling for the sons to beg the widow of a man whom they had been taught to despise all their lives and that too, for this petty favour in order to arrange a decent funeral for their father in this 'alien' place. At the same time I consider it a day of great significance for our family, when through her humanitarian gesture of extending to the 'enemy' the temporary hospitality of her kitchen, mother was able to impose this legacy of moral debt on behalf of her husband's clan on the offspring of his rival for all time to come.

However, it must be said that there was nothing outwardly extraordinary about father's short life; but the respect he inspired in his fellow villagers and relatives alike is still a part of our village lore. I attribute this to the age-old 'sense of self' that ordinary rural folk cherish as the bed-rock of their simple existence. Father took pride in his own 'sense of self' and derived his moral strength from the belief that no power on earth could deprive him of his history, heritage and rightful place in society. Even as I write this, the jolt of pain I felt when I first heard of people actually celebrating father's death so many years ago comes back afresh. But I rejoice that I am the daughter of such a man. Our parents did not leave us any material legacy; but what we inherited from them is this priceless sense of belief in our intrinsic worth. And if there is any lesson to be learnt from their ordinary lives, it is this: political power may prevail for a time, what money can buy is always relative; they all pass. But the truth about lineage and heritage on the other hand is unassailable and is therefore incorruptible by unscrupulous men and their machinations.

The understanding of these perceptions about our parents' lives would later provide the right context for the various

destinies of their children. But when they died within the
short span of nine months, all that we inherited at that point
of time was a legacy of colossal personal loss that haunted
our individual lives. That we overcame such a legacy and
survived is a miracle that is still playing out in our lives.

Orphans at Large: The Wild Days

Not very long after mother's death the first split-up in our
family happened because the initial baby-sitting visits of
the friendly nurses had to be curtailed on account of their
own strict and tight schedules of classes and ward duties.
Since there would be no one to babysit our younger sister
and youngest brother anymore, who needed constant
supervision, it was decided that they were to be taken to
our ancestral village where our various aunts and maternal
grandmother would look after them by turns. The two elder
brothers, I, and the younger brother were left in the house
which was allotted to father perhaps to complete that school
year. On the surface there was a semblance of 'family' in the
familiar surroundings and with siblings in the same house.
But the true cohesion of such a unit and protection for it that
only a parent or parents can give was not there; we were
not a 'family' any more, only a bunch of orphans left in the
old house to fend for ourselves as best as we could. Even
among the four of us, there was a disparity in our ages. Our
two elder brothers were already in High School whereas the
two of us were still in Primary School. So our daily routines
were vastly different and we were left mainly to our own
devices after our classes were over. And even if we did not
go to school regularly, our brothers would normally not
know anything about our activities because they were away
from home for most of the day. On the whole we must have
appeared a most pathetic lot and were often described by

our relatives and fellow villagers as 'helpless chicks after the mother hen has been snatched away by a hawk'. But at the same time for the two of us, my younger brother Along and I, it also meant a measure of freedom to do whatever we liked with our time and with our elder brothers away from home most of the day, we two soon lost our way.

Initial memories from this period of life are mostly about absconding from school in the company of older girls, roaming the paddy fields, digging up some wild roots and eating them. I liked the company of these older girls because they seemed to be so knowledgeable about everything and because they talked freely about all manner of things including the various boys in the compound and what they thought about them. At first they were reluctant to take me along with them on their excursions but eventually they relented and allowed me to accompany them wherever they went. Once we went to the house of an old lady who lived just outside the compound, because one of the girls wanted to have her ear pierced again because the original hole had closed up somehow. I watched the proceedings in great fascination as the earlobe was massaged with some liquid for a few minutes. Then the old woman began to chat, perhaps to distract the girl's attention for she was beginning to show signs of tension. While rubbing the earlobe with her potion, she said that even the morning dew helps numb the lobe so that the prick of the needle is not so painful. Before anyone knew what was happening, she jabbed the needle on the spot she had chosen right into the cork held behind the lobe. As she pulled the cork away, the thread attached to the needle also came through. There was hardly any bleeding. The girl cried a bit but as she was tying the knot on the thread, the old woman consoled her by saying, 'Don't cry, it's just a little prick. Just think, you can now wear beautiful earrings'. She instructed the girl not to scratch even if there was itching and said that the thread had to be pulled back and forth regularly with the help of a little oil dabbed on the hole to enlarge it.

I began to think about this when I went home. Though I had both ears pierced, the hole on my left ear was higher than the one on the right and when I wore earrings, the one on the left ear would skew out on the side making me look funny. I tried pulling it back to make it dangle straight down but it would not stay that way long because of the position of the hole. I decided that I needed a new hole in my left ear. After a few days, early one morning I slipped out of the house and went to this old woman's house. When she came out of her house, I asked her if she would pierce a new hole on my left ear. She looked me up and down and said that I would have to pay her two annas for the job. I said that I had no money. She looked sterner than before and said, 'Go away, come only when you have the money' and shut the door in my face.

I was both angry and also humiliated but this only sharpened my desire to have a proper hole on my left ear. But I knew that I could never find the two annas to pay the old woman for doing this; I had to find a way myself. It was then that I decided to pierce my own ear. I started collecting the necessary things for the job: a biggish needle, sturdy thread, a piece of cork and of course a mirror. I hid all these things from my brothers and early one morning, I went behind the kitchen with the 'equipment'. I was hesitant at first and a bit afraid too. But then having gone to all the trouble and knowing that I could never have the money to pay the old woman to do the piercing, I could not back out now. Besides, I wanted to show her that she was not the only one who could pierce a hole in the ear. I gathered dew from the grass, smeared it on my left ear and began rubbing it in. When the ear was cold enough, I peered into the small mirror and put a dot on the lobe for the new hole. Then I gritted my teeth and pushed the needle into the spot and when it lodged on the cork I pulled it back slowly and eventually the thread came through the ear! There, I had done it, I was jubilant. After several tries I could secure the two ends into a knot. I kept the thread looped through the hole for sometime, always pulling it back and forth as the old woman had instructed. I will not say that it did not hurt; and the wound also festered a bit but soon subsided into scabs which I removed daily. And one day when I no longer felt any pain when I 'exercised' the thread in my ear, I cut off the knot and pulled it out. My ear felt alright and I immediately tried my only pair of dangling earrings and what a delight, the left one no longer jutted out of alignment! This is how I managed to have three holes, one on the right and two on my left ear. The original hole on the left ear has almost disappeared due to disuse but the new one I created for myself has displayed many a dangling trinket during my heyday and has now quietly settled down to anchor the more sedate ones befitting my age!

There were days when I could not be with the older girls and I would try to accompany my younger brother's friends on their fishing trips or tree-climbing jaunts. They would discourage me by saying that girls cannot do these things. But I followed them regardless and sometimes out of extreme annoyance they would throw pebbles at me shouting, 'Go away, we don't want girls, they bring bad luck'. But I obstinately followed them because I had nowhere else to go: the older girls were not around and children my age would either be in school or in their homes with their parents. No matter how much they resented my presence among them, the boys were stuck with me. To ensure that I would not be shooed off, I volunteered to carry their fishing rods as well as the tin cans which held the slimy worms they used as bait. Sometimes the worms would slither on to my hands and I would shriek. Once I even dropped the tin and the worms were crawling every which way in a bid to escape. Cursing me loudly, the boys helped gather the wriggling mass and put a leaf cover on the tin. It was a disgusting job but I continued with the hateful task because I did not want to be left alone in the house.

There was another thing which the boys thought only they could do: climbing trees. But I had other ideas and started to climb trees whenever they indulged in tree-climbing games. In order to become as skilful as them, I started shimmying up the guava tree behind our house when I was alone. I became quite good at it and began to enjoy the experience, especially when I could climb up and pluck the ripe guavas in season and eat to my heart's content. But one day one of the boys found out what I was doing and said that no girl could be as good a tree-climber as a boy. I said I could prove him wrong. Ok then, he said, we would play 'catch me' on the tree to test who was right. The one who was the 'it' would jump from branch to branch in order not to be caught by the others on the other branches. In the beginning I was always 'caught' but by and by I became quite an expert at evading their touch by jumping to the next branch and eluding their pursuit. I was quite small compared to them and guava branches, even the small ones are very sturdy. But they are smooth and slippery too.

During one such game day we were jumping madly from branch to branch shrieking loudly when all on a sudden I found my grip on a high branch slipping and I fell to the hard ground with a big thud. Everything went black for me, it felt as though a big stone was pressing down on my chest and I could not breathe. They told me afterwards that I had 'died' for the few minutes that I had lain inert on the ground and also added how scared they were. How I came to or who helped me is a total blank and we never played that particular game again. But in spite of that near-death experience I still remember that it was great fun when we played 'catch me' on the guava tree and jumped from branch to branch like a noisy pack of monkeys!

It was during these wild days that I nearly drowned in the stream that was quite close to our compound. It was a Sunday and we were supposed to go to Sunday School; but when we started walking towards the Chapel, one of my brother's friends stopped and said, 'Hey I saw some ripe berries on the other side of the stream, why don't we pluck them first?' No one said a word: skipping Sunday School would surely be reported and everyone was afraid. But he continued, 'See, we can run across the stream, pluck and eat the berries and run back to the Chapel, it won't take long if we hurry now'. So saying he turned and ran towards the stream and slid down the bank and crossed over in no time at all. The bigger boys followed but I could not keep pace and lagged behind. In order to catch up with them, I chose a different spot to cross the stream and was caught in an eddy; I began to sink. My brother looked back and began to scream, 'she's drowning, she's drowning'. Hearing his screams a big boy jumped to where I was and was just in time to grab my thick hair to which he held on and with the help of the others pulled me to the bank. By that time I had drunk lots of water and the moment my body hit the ground I began to puke, the muddy water gushing out in painful gasps. I could not stand, let alone walk. The rest of the day is a blur. But from that time on I developed a mortal fear of water and of course I never learnt to swim either.

During this period one day my brother and I experimented with a real cigarette. How we got hold of it I cannot recall now but we were both excited. We crept behind the latrine shed and he somehow lit it; we then started puffing on it by turn, coughing after every drag and laughing. Unfortunately for us, our eldest brother came home unexpectedly early that day and when he did not find us at home, came out to investigate. Following the ruckus we were making, he caught us red-handed and we must have been punished for our folly but honestly I cannot recall in what way. What I do remember is the horrid taste of the cigarette and the nausea which stayed for quite some time. My experiments with tobacco, the first time with the village woman's pipe and now the cigarette both ended in a fiasco.

It may sound funny but though indifferent to smoking ever since these unpleasant experiences, there is one particular tobacco smell which is as pleasant as the other two were not: the Capstan smell. I remember seeing a round tin from where the tobacco was extracted. It would then be mashed on the palm for sometime and then rolled into a cigarette in thin white paper. The aroma of the tobacco would fill the room when it was lighted and I seemed to like it. Who did that and when I cannot recall; all that has stayed in my mind is the rich aroma which seemed to linger on. Would I have liked to experiment with that? I have no answer to that. That particular method of rolling a cigarette must have been overtaken by the ready made ones. In later years I did ask some smokers if they'd tasted such rolled Capstan cigarettes and each one spoke nostalgically about the richness of the tobacco that I too remember. I often wonder if my younger brother too remembers the Capstan aroma or our escapade with the cigarette, he who gave up serious smoking after indulging in it for about twenty years of his adult life.

Day of Reckoning

The fact that both my brother and I were staying away from school was eventually discovered by our eldest brother and one evening we were hauled up before him. We were always in awe of this brother who spoke so little, only gave orders and saw to it that there was some food for us in the house. That evening he called out for us taking our full names and we trembled because whenever we were summoned in this manner, we knew that we were in big trouble. Without any preamble, he took up a cane and began hitting us. Luckily for us there were some relatives who were visiting us and they saved us from the hiding of our lives. From then on, of course, playing truant from school did not appeal to us so much and though we hated it, especially I, because by that time I was enrolled in the Jorhat Girls' School in town which was some three miles from home and we had to walk there and back every day of the week except Sundays and holidays. When I remember the few lashes on my calf that day, I still shudder to think of what might have happened if the elderly relatives had not intervened. The walk to school in the heat was an ordeal but the prospect of another hiding was more dreadful; so I became more regular in my attendance.

The situation on the home front seems to have gone from bad to worse; some days we would go to school on empty stomachs because there was either no food to cook or even if there was a little rice, the firewood would be so raw and damp that I could not light the fire at all. Those were miserable days. If a school mate gave me a few grains of chana I would devour them greedily and wash it down with water from the school tap. It is still a mystery how we survived this impossible period. Once it was so bad that I decided to go to our paternal aunt's house in the Police Reserve a few miles from our house to beg her to give us some food. Her situation was not much better: her husband was a mere constable in the Assam Police and they had five children. It so turned out that they were eating only one meal a day during that period. But seeing our hungry look and emaciated frames, she must have taken pity on us and gave us about half a kilogram of atta from the ration they got that day from the Depot. She put it in a paper bag and instructed me to be careful while we walked back home. It was already evening and not only that, we had to walk by the front of the town jail right across the main road. Whenever we passed this way on earlier occasions to her house I would feel extremely fearful of the two sentries always standing in front of the massive door. They wore red turban-like hats with tassels falling to one side of their neck, khaki shorts and black boots. The most frightening things about them were the guns they held on their right shoulders, looking as if at any moment they would fire the deadly weapon at passers-by. But it was the only road and we had to pass them on our way home. Trying to muster as much false courage as possible, I held my younger brother's hand and keeping him close to me we walked fast and somehow crossed that dreadful space.

But with the atta we were not so lucky: it began to rain and no matter how much I tried to shield the packet of atta, the rain eventually won. By the time we got home, all that was left of the precious gift aunty gave us, was the soggy paper bag from which the wet dough had oozed out and dripped on to the roadside. Some of it still clung to my drenched frock when we finally reached home. All dreams of eating at least a hot chapatti that evening were thus washed away by the rain. That night too, we went to bed hungry. It was no consolation that it was not the first night that we had to go to bed on an empty stomach. I cannot recall how many such nights we had to endure.

This also reminds me of an incident after our parents' death. One Sunday, there was a feast in the senior doctor's house in the hospital compound where we lived then, and many people were invited. We, my brother and I, knew what was going on, but not being invited we dared not go to the feast. Our elder brothers had gone out and there was no food in the house. We waited for them to come home and cook but till mid-afternoon, there was no sign of them. We were hungry and as if propelled by the prospect of food, we crept to the fence of the doctor's house and peeped through the hedge at the activities in the open backyard. The lady of the house was doling out food to the assorted servants and attendants from huge dekchis and the aroma of cooked rice and meat curry wafted to where we crouched and we became hungrier. We thought we were invisible but someone saw us and reported to the lady who beckoned to us; at first we were ashamed to face the crowd, but the hunger was so overwhelming and the prospect of food so tempting that we shuffled our way to the line squatting on the ground and joined them in eating the food served by the lady. Of course the rice was from the bottom of the pot and slightly burnt. But it was more than compensated by the gravy of the meat curry. We even got to eat a few pieces of actual meat! Even while we were eating, there was a nagging feeling in my mind about our presence in the company of the workers. Young though I was, I was aware of the sense of 'shame' in eating the food we were not invited for. But the memory of the meal we ate that day still remains in my mind as the best meal I tasted in a long while. On our way back home, my brother and I vowed to each other that we would never tell our elder brothers that we went to the doctor's feast as uninvited guests, as beggars and enjoyed the meal of left-over delicacies. Luckily for us, they never found out why we refused to eat the simple dinner they cooked that night.

But then there were some days when our eldest brother would bring home rice and meat and cook a delicious meal for all four of us. But such good days were few and far between. Another break during this 'lean' period was the coming of 'guests', relatives from the village who came to the town on personal errands. They would invariably come to stay in

our house because it was convenient and free and my elder
brothers would help them out by taking them to the right
shops or meet the right doctors in the hospital. The coming
of guests meant good food because it is a custom among us
that when one travels, he or she carries enough provisions
like rice, dry meat etc. to last the number of days they intend
to stay away. And knowing that our house was a house of
orphans, they would always carry extra provisions for us too.
We felt happy when such guests came to our house to stay
because their coming meant good food and therefore they
were always welcome!

In spite of the hardship at home, I was quite happy at
school and was learning fast. I could read and write better
than the others. Seeing my progress, my eldest brother
decided to teach me the English alphabet. Normally in
Assam those days this was taught only from class IV. I was
a fast learner and very soon I was looking for English books
to test my new-found skill, but the only books in English
around the house were the Bible and some hymn books. My
brothers' books were of course out of bounds for me. It was
then that I decided to go to English service every Sunday
evening in the chapel where I held the English hymnals
and pretended to sing along with the others. I am sure that
I became a source of much amusement to the others who
saw through my pretence but for me these meetings were
important because even if I could not read the verses to sing
along, I could memorize the chorus of many of the songs
which are repeated after every verse. That way in subsequent
services when some of these were chosen for the evening, I
sang the loudest when the chorus was repeated!

Before I joined the school in town, we normally walked
in a group to our school in the hospital campus which was
situated right next to the gate leading from the main road.
And every morning the subject of our discussion was what

we should do if we met the white sahib on his way to the hospital coming from the opposite direction. We were in mortal awe of this huge man, who had the reputation of being short-tempered. Even the adults, nurses and other doctors alike were afraid of him, we were told. The few times we met him on our way to school, all of us slid away from the elevated road and walked on its lower perimeter, quickening our pace. The sahib would walk past us in his hulking way without even a sideway glance at us.

One day I suggested to my friends that instead of acting like cowards, we should say 'Good Morning' to him and see what he does. They were aghast and thought that I had gone crazy. But I kept at them for many days and finally one of them asked who was going to say it to him? I said, 'all of us.' They shrieked, No. "Alright then, I will say it' I retorted and it was decided that the very first time we met him after this, I would greet him with a 'Good Morning' on the condition that they all stayed close to me.

After two days of this momentous decision, we saw him at a distance coming out of his gate and walking towards us. It was the moment of truth; the expected 'confrontation' would show if I could hold my ground and redeem my promise given in such a foolhardy manner. As he stepped closer and I was rehearsing my good morning silently, I suddenly became aware that all the others had slunk away to the lower road and I was the lone walker going to meet the giant. I was trembling inwardly but tried not to show it and as we came parallel to each other I croaked at him, 'Good morning sir'. He looked at me and gave me a faint smile before he shuffled off. I stood rooted on the spot, angry with the others but gloating inside that I'd taken a dare without running away like my friends.

Meanwhile in school we were being prepared for the Board exams at the end of class III. I was quite confident about the other subjects but the drawing class always put me in a spot. Besides, I was the only one without the coloured crayons we were supposed to have for this class. I did not know what to do. I thought over it and decided that the only solution was to go and ask the memsahib to help me out with the discards of her children which may still be usable. So mustering all my courage, the next day I went to the bungalow gate and told the chowkidar that I wanted to meet the lady. He asked me why but I did not say anything. I just stood there as he glared at me. Fortunately for me, just at that moment the lady appeared carrying a plate of sweet rotis for her children and their friends who were playing near the gate. She saw me and called me inside and gave me two of the rotis. I ate them hungrily. After giving the plate to her children, she took me aside and wanted to know why I had come to see her. When she heard what I needed, she smiled and asked me to wait. She went upstairs and soon came down with a packet of brand new crayons and handed it to me. I was delighted and ran home without saying anything to her. I do not remember whether I actually used them in the exam or if I really needed them in the first place. But I always remember the generosity of this lady with an immense sense of gratitude.

My progress in school was good and I was learning new things every day. By now I could read and write the Assamese language quite well. I remember an incident of a different nature where my reading and writing skills came in handy. I somehow got befriended by a much older girl who was living in a nearby village just outside the hospital compound. She often used to call me to her home and give me snacks and fruits etc. One day she sent for me and after some hesitation said that she had an important task for me. But she made me promise first that I would not tell anybody about what she was going to show me. I promised, and then she brought out a letter from the front of her blouse and asked me to read it for her because she was illiterate. It was a letter from her boyfriend, she said. I became both terrified and excited because by that time being in the company of older girls and exposed to their conversations, I was no longer ignorant about the facts of life and what happens between boys and girls. And I also knew that letters from boyfriends could be dangerous for both the receiver and the reader. But on this occasion, my curiosity overcame my initial trepidation. When I still hesitated, the girl, as if she could sense what I was thinking, pointed out that I was already an accomplice because I had looked at the letter and had even taken the oath of secrecy.

So I read the letter aloud to her though I do not remember what I read. The girl then said that she wanted to send a reply. I knew I was getting deeper into trouble but there was no way out at this stage. So reluctantly and with dread, I began to write what she dictated. It took quite a while because she wanted changes several times and I had to oblige. When it was finished, she asked me to read it back to her and she seemed to be satisfied. She then said that she would take the letter herself. I pointed out that she had to sign it, otherwise how would he know who the letter was from? She stood there for a while thinking and then asked me to write her name for her. I was beginning to get annoyed with this big girl who was going to put me in trouble if the letter was ever discovered by her father or somebody else. She urged me on and after signing her name, on a sudden and mad impulse, I added something naughty: I wrote 'kisses', a word I heard from the big girls, on the margin below her name, folded it neatly and gave the letter to the happy girl. I waited until she sealed it and tucked it inside her blouse along with the other letter. As payment perhaps for writing the letter, she gave me some food which I ate hungrily and then I walked home slowly, vowing to myself that I would never ever get mixed up with this girl or anyone like her and inwardly hoped that her letter containing my mischief, would never reach the boy. To this day I do not know what happened to the girl or the letter I wrote on her behalf because soon after this incident her family moved away from the village.

Throughout this period of our life, hunger was an ever-present reality and it seemed that we went hungry most days or had just one meal a day. But then I came across a class-mate, a Muslim girl whose behaviour at a certain period of the year completely turned my idea of hunger upside down.

I was not close to her and barely spoke to her once or twice when we happened to go to the water tap outside at the same time. We used to sit on long benches wherever there was space and one day we found ourselves sitting next to each other. I gradually became aware that at regular intervals she would go out and come back after a minute or two. I became curious, but what puzzled me more was that the teacher did not say anything to her at all about these frequent visits outside. Unable to contain my curiosity, I walked up to her during recess and asked her what she did when she went out of the classroom. She said she spat out saliva. I asked her why she didn't simply swallow it. She said she was observing a fast for one whole month and it was against her religion to swallow even saliva during this period. I then asked her if she also went to bed hungry. She laughed and said no, after sunset they could eat anything and as much as they liked; it was only during the daytime that they could not eat anything, not even swallow their own spit. I was amazed beyond words to learn that people actually inflicted hunger on themselves in the name of religion! This hunger was so totally different from the devastating kind we were experiencing, days on end sometimes. But for this girl and others following the same religion it was not hunger at all; it was simply a ritual for the daytime with the redeeming assurance of food at nightfall. She also told me that before sunrise everyone in the family ate as much as they could so that they would not feel faint during the day. Reflecting on it now, it amazes me to realize how one type of hunger had so much significance whereas the hunger we experienced seemed so cruel and meaningless.

If physical hunger was becoming the order of our existence, there was another kind of deprivation that was beginning to have its toll on us. My only constant companion during that period was my younger brother. But we found ourselves getting into quarrels very frequently. For example, when we went to bed, (we slept on the same bed), a game would start innocuously like 'don't touch me'. But one of us would surreptitiously touch the other and would be touched back with whispered protest. But the irritating touches would be exchanged until a retaliatory touch would become a hard slap. Then another hard slap in return, with shouts of 'I said don't touch me' and the game would suddenly turn into an earnest fist fight, then the pillows would fly amid more screaming and pulling of hair, eyes, ears and the stronger one would react with blows. Instead of falling asleep quietly, we would find ourselves in the middle of a genuine physical encounter with each other. This may have been because often we had to go to bed hungry or with very little food. Or some inner rage that sought release would make us behave in this manner at the slightest provocation. We would fall asleep only after we were physically and mentally exhausted.

I remember a night when our eldest brother heard us screaming and told us to shut up and go to bed. But our fight continued and he, in his anger and frustration perhaps, pulled us out of the bed and threw us into the wood shed outside. It cooled us down but we were now stranded in the darkness and became thoroughly terrified. We had to scramble to the top of the pile of scratchy stumps of wood in the dark as far away from the open door as possible for fear of ghosts or wild animals. I do not remember how long the banishment lasted; an hour or more or the whole night. These bed-time scuffles may have appeared as childish squabbles gone bad but actually they were the first signs that our existence as a family was fast crumbling. The two of us were left more and more to our devices and as a result we began associating with all kinds of people in and around the compound and were becoming quite unruly. We once accompanied a group of Nepali cowherds to see a movie in the town without our brothers' permission or knowledge because they were not around. I remember walking back from the town in pitch darkness and how the hot tarmac of the road burnt into our bare soles.

It was not the fault of our brothers that things were going this way. In all fairness to them it must be understood that they too were struggling to cope with their own studies and the pitiable condition in the house. In order to earn some pocket money they would hire themselves out to football teams which played all over the town and in tea gardens beyond. Sometimes they would come home all dirty and many times with injuries. They may have been much older than the two of us, but it was an enormous responsibility for them to keep the family properly fed and housed on top of coping with their own problems and keeping us on track. The house we lived in was also was beginning to fall apart: the thatch roof leaked in many places, doors and windows were coming off their hinges and it remained unswept for days on end. Though we shifted our beds constantly, the rain would eventually find these spots too and many nights we had to sleep on wet mattresses because they could not be dried on account of the rains. They soon rotted and stank and eventually were thrown out, replacements being out of the question. Though so young, it became my responsibility to cook most of the time just because I was a girl. The result was often disastrous: the rice would either be half-cooked or burnt and there would be another hungry day for all of us. It was becoming clear to all that that the family of orphans was disintegrating and unless something was done to salvage their lives, there was a greater tragedy awaiting them in the imminent future.

Perhaps it was on account of this factor that some decision must have been taken about our re-location. As a result of this, my younger brother was to be sent to the village to study there along with the two youngest siblings who were already there. And I was to be sent to a boarding school in the plains to continue my studies. It was thus that even the semblance of a family that survived my parents' death through these hardships for some time finally disappeared and we were separated from each other. We were to remain dislocated in this manner for many years and in fact we never really came together as a family unit ever again. It was only after we made our various ways in life somehow and had our own individual families, that the notion of a family became a reality for us.

We literally grew up without really savouring of the comforting warmth of love and care from parents. I honestly do not know in a very conscious way, what it is to be loved by a father or mother and it has been extremely painful to have grown to maturity with this deprivation. It is this emotional dislocation that had left all six of us terribly maimed in spirit and soul. Though we all have children of our own and have tried to give them as much love and care as we know how, I cannot honestly say how far we have succeeded in our roles as parents. If the 'giving' has left something 'wanting', I can only say that not receiving the same when we needed it most must have created an emotional vacuum in us which may have left its debilitating stamp on our various psyches.

But life has an amazing way of compensating its own lapses and perhaps the decision to dismantle the disfunctional family of orphans and sending them all in different directions was the defining moment which launched us into our individual destinies. It was from this point of time onward that our various stories would be scripted by the circumstances in which we were placed. The three younger siblings were now taken in by my youngest paternal uncle while my brother Tajen got a job in the village Primary School after his Matriculation and so the four of them had a semblance of family life in uncle's house along with our cousins. My eldest brother managed to pass the Intermediate Examination from a college in Jorhat and went on to become a petty clerk in a government office in the then Naga Hills District of Assam. While in service he successfully completed his graduation. That was the beginning of his long and successful career as a Civil Servant in the Nagaland Government. He was conferred the IAS and went on to become Secretary/Commissioner and retired in due course. After retirement also he served as an Advisor to the Government for a number of years. My brother Tajen remained in the village as a teacher and went on to receive the President's Medal for meritorious service as a teacher. He also became the custodian of our family's interests there. After his retirement he became a public leader of considerable repute and served as Chairman of the Village Council of Changki for more than two terms.

But the journey to these modest personal heights was tortuous for all of us. We had to endure hardships and frustrations all along the way. However, as far as the emotional dislocation was concerned, it would appear that I was the most affected on account of being away from the others for six long years. Our reunions were few and far between during the years following this dislocation. It also meant that whereas earlier, there was a collective sense of loss, now I was the one destined to bear this all by myself away from the familiar environment. Therefore the most important segment in the story of my life centres on the six years that I spent in a boarding school trying to cope with the enormous burden of 'alone-ness' and 'abandonment'.

But before I go to that period of my life, I need to talk about something else first. It may sound incongruous, but there are two distinct recollections of 'things' from this period of our life which have remained vivid in my memory all these years.

The first is a gramophone, the kind that had a duck-neck-shaped head where you inserted a pin each time you wanted to 'play' a record. The head was fixed on a box-like contraption which had an opening at the back. And it was this hole which fascinated me the most. I used to insert my hand into it thinking that perhaps I could touch the singers hidden in the cave-like space who were producing the lovely songs! And I wondered how so many people could fit into so small a space. I also remember that somewhere on the machine there was a picture of a dog.

Sometimes when the voices coming from the record sounded scratchy, they would say, change the pin. And when we ran out of fresh pins, they would make us the younger ones, sharpen the short pin-ends on a stone surface. If the pin was too blunt and you still let it play on the record, then it created dents and spoiled the record. Like our dislocated lives, this gramophone also was abandoned somewhere along the way. But while it worked, it provided us with some sweet and short intervals of lovely melodies in an otherwise dull existence.

The other memory is from my short stint in class IV in the Government Girls' School in Jorhat. What I remember vividly about our class in this school is strangely, not any teacher or class-mate but the overhead cloth fan that hung from a high beam in the centre of the ceiling! There was a long rope attached to it which had to be pulled. There was a woman whose job it was to pull it back and forth during our classes so that the cool air would relieve us from the oppressive heat of summer. Before the coming of electric fans and air-conditioners such 'pullers' must have been indispensable in any rich home or government institution. Sometimes when the teacher was absent, this woman would refuse to pull the contraption saying that her arms hurt from tugging at the heavy cloth fan for long hours. Then some of us would try pulling it and that is how we found out how heavy it indeed was. No one uses these contraptions anymore though a few more richly decorated ones can still be seen in old havelis around the country as ornamental furnishings in addition to modern fittings and also perhaps as reminders of the owners' princely past. And the more ornate version of the kind of gramophone I remember has now become a collector's item. It is amazing how human beings tend to re-signify their past possessions in their present context.

These are some of the memories of my early life but with the eventual dispersal of the siblings, the time had come for me to move on to a new location where I would have to adjust to a completely new environment. It was as if I would be transplanted in the fresh soil of a new school to live with a hundred other girls as a family. It was a bewildering prospect but until I actually started life in the school and hostel, I could not imagine how momentous the transition was going to be. All that I was aware of at this particular point of time was that I was being sent to a strange place away from my siblings. I do not remember if I was disturbed about this fact at all; it was all so vague, the sudden flurry of activities in the house, relatives coming and going. I was young and naïve and could not fully grasp the significance of this re-location. It is only hind-sight that convinces me that in fact it was this event which introduced me to this new environment and which proved to be my 'emancipation' from a very difficult childhood where the future had looked so hopeless. The transition was not easy and would entail many hardships of a different nature but as it turned out, the experience turned out to be invaluable. The education I received here and the discipline I learnt to accept helped me to forge a new future for myself.

PART II

PART II

A New Beginning

On a cold January morning, I found myself within the compound of the Ridgeway Girls' High School, Golaghat in Assam, brought there, most probably by my elder brother. I do not remember if I said goodbye to my younger brother who would later be sent to the village. But I distinctly remember that the two of us had stood in front of the fireplace watching a chicken curry being cooked the night before. At one stage when I put something into the big karhai, there was a big whoosh and the contents caught fire! We both jumped back and I somehow picked up the lid and covered the dish and the fire went out. Curiously enough I do not remember eating any of it.

Nor do I remember how we travelled from Jorhat to this place or if there were any goodbyes exchanged before my brother seemed to disappear from my life. I did not know it at that time but I would not see him for the next two or three years. And little did I realize then that this circumscribed space was going to be my 'home' for the next six years and that I was embarking on a new phase which was to change the direction of my life forever. The only conscious memory of that re-location was the deep sense of being truly 'orphaned', away from my siblings and the familiar environment of my troubled childhood. When I look back on this momentous change in my life, what amazes me is the fact that though I was the object of the planning, I seem to have remained anonymous in the process that placed me in this new environment.

The reason for my being put in this school must have
been this: I was studying in class IV in an Assamese medium
school and our village school was not suitable for me because
everything was taught in our vernacular. I had to be sent
to a school where I could continue my studies under the
same syllabus. But the timing of my transfer was all wrong.
The annual examinations were due in two months' time and
my schooling since my parents' death had been minimal to
say the least. Because I was already in class IV in my old
school, I was put in the same class in the new school. That
first year was a nightmare for me which began the moment
I saw what the others in the class were doing. In the first
place the standard of my old school could never match this
one, classes were held in right earnest here and the teachers
were hard task-masters. In the old school I did not even
know what books were to be studied and even if I was told,
I could have never bought them. To my utter horror I found
out that my classmates were even reading English texts and
had nearly completed all the work-books in English whereas
I had barely learnt the alphabets.

If things looked grim at school, life in the hostel was
equally harsh, if not worse. All the cooking, sweeping,
cleaning and washing of dishes were to be done by the
hostellers themselves. They were housed in different
buildings simply called Houses each with a number. Every
House had an in-charge known as Mahi, which means
mother's younger sister in Assamese. It was her job to assign
duties to all the residents on a weekly routine. There would
be head cooks, assisted by some junior cooks whose job was
to scrub the huge utensils, wash the cups and plates, sweep
and mop the kitchen floor after meals. Lunch would have
to be ready by 8 am so that the kitchen could be made spic
and span before going to school by 9 am. In the House itself
there would be others who had to sweep the rooms, each

girl had to make her own bed and tidy up before going to school. During school hours the rooms and kitchens would be 'inspected' by the Matron of the hostel and any House which did not meet the required standard of cleanliness and tidiness would be 'punished'.

It was a bewildering environment into which I was plunged so suddenly. I found myself among girls of different ages from different backgrounds and it soon became clear to me that I was one of the youngest among these strangers. Young as I was, some instinct must have made me realize that I had to survive in this school and hostel; I had to learn how to cope with the new reality. But even now I remember how lost I used to feel among so many. If before coming to this school I had felt deprived of parental love and the comfort of being in a regular home, I had at least my brothers for company who were in the same circumstances. But here in this new situation I was all alone and there was no one who would understand my feelings even if I told them and that made me feel all the more isolated. It was a terribly lonely struggle especially the first few months but I had to learn how to survive in this new environment. Besides, the systems in the school as well as the hostel were such that days passed swiftly with mechanical precision and we had to fall into our assigned positions like automatons. As I slowly fitted into the routine, I began to realize that if there was to be any redemption from my present predicament, it would only be through hard work in the hostel and success in studies. The more I began to believe in this the more determined I became to excel at my studies. And that was the only glimmer of hope in an otherwise bleak and uncertain future.

As I look back on this very difficult period of adjustment, I feel that at that point of time, my previous life seemed to have been wiped clean and I had to begin on a blank page. My first experiences in the new environment were disastrous. To begin with, on the third day after I joined the hostel, I committed a 'crime'. That day being a Saturday we had no school and it was also a 'Visitors' day. I was bored and also curious to know what was happening; so I quietly walked towards the Super's bungalow to see what was going on. No one noticed my presence but after a little while, a visitor spotted me loitering and asked me to call his daughter whose name I have now forgotten, from the hostel. Eager to be of some help, I ran to the hostel and told the girl that someone wanted to see her and was waiting in front of Miss's bungalow. She hopped away happily only to be stopped and scolded by the Super who had by now come out to the verandah. When asked how she knew her father was here, she told her that I was the one who called her.

What followed afterwards still remains the most hurtful and humiliating experience of my hostel life. I was hauled up before the Super and for my 'crime' of calling the girl without her permission I was to be punished because I had broken a hostel rule. I was made to sweep the compound in front of the bungalow where many more visitors had arrived by then. I swept for almost an hour and gathered the leaves and other debris in a heap which I had to carry to the dump. I did not mind the physical punishment, but what pained me most was the public humiliation in front of so many visitors simply because of my ignorance of hostel rules. The Super did not consider the fact that I had been in the hostel for only three days and if she wanted to teach me a lesson, perhaps a stern verbal warning would have sufficed. Though I regretted my own action, I felt a strong sense of resentment against the Super for treating me so unfairly. This antagonistic attitude was to remain in my mind throughout the six years that I was in this school and it seems to have formed the nucleus of a running feud between her and me which erupted time and again during my stay in the hostel.

There was another incident during my early days in the hostel, on another Saturday. In a small room in one of the Houses, there were four of us, all juniors. The bed next to mine belonged to a girl called Winnie. Earlier in the day her mother had come to visit her and she looked very happy, as did all the others who had visitors. After lights-out that evening, the Matron entered our room on her regular 'patrols', I got scared because I was still nervous from my 'punishment' on an earlier Saturday and wondered if I had done something wrong again. I held my breath. But on entering the quiet room, she heard some rustling from the next bed and when she pulled the quilt back she found Winnie munching on a paratha that her mother had sneaked in. Hostellers were not allowed to receive any food-stuff even from parents and Winnie had violated the rule. I still remember the Matron scolding her; but surprisingly not for breaking the rule but for not sharing the food with me! I was scared for Winnie but I do not think that she was punished at all. After the Matron left, we looked at each other in the semi-dark room and something must have connected because from this incident onwards she and I became very good friends though she was a class senior to me. The Matron's words comforted me somehow, knowing that there was at least someone who cared how I must have I felt at Winnie's selfish behaviour.

Burnt Curry

There was however no time to mope around once I became a hosteller, and being the youngest in my House, I was assigned to kitchen duty as a junior cook. It was an enormous burden for the cooks of the week who had to cope with heavy homework from school, sometimes having to forego the much needed bath in the bargain, but as I learnt immediately there was a huge bonus for them. The food was doled out by the cooks into plates owned by the girls; the menu was very simple. Often it would be rice and dal for lunch and rice and one curry, mostly of the cheapest vegetables like brinjal, pumpkin, ladies' fingers, gourd etc. for dinner. More often than not, the rice would be burnt at the bottom of the huge utensil; cooking rice for around twenty-five persons in a single dish on a raw wood fire often resulted in either the rice getting burnt or some remaining half-cooked. No matter: it was a prize for the cooks! After the curry was doled out, they would scrape the burnt rice from the bottom of the pot into the big karhai, where some burnt curry clung at the bottom, and mix the two and make them into balls, one for each of the cooks. This was the coveted extra which made the onerous job of the cooks bearable! This was an open secret and anyone who dared tattle to the Matron about this would be appropriately 'punished' by the cooks. Her plate would either be missing on certain days or she would find a lump of hair in her rice!

I do not remember what the extra ball of burnt rice and curry tasted like but during my stint as a junior cook, it was always the high point of my day when there was an additional lump of food on my tin plate. It was hard work scrubbing the soot from huge degchis and karhais but this extra food was gratefully accepted by a stomach which remained hungry throughout the six years of my stay in this boarding school.

Talking about hunger: if in my earlier life hunger was a constant and ever present threat, here in this new environment the one comfort was knowing that two square meals, however bland were assured. On the other hand whereas studies were only in the periphery of my earlier existence, they had to become the sole purpose of my being here and as time went by, my resolve to excel at them grew stronger.

As I recount this, I remember an incident while on a visit to our village one winter when I saw my aunt doling out burnt rice to her servants and was made to believe that such rice was meant for servants and pigs only. But here I was looking forward to my next stint as junior cook in the beginning and as senior cook in high school when I could devour a ball of burnt rice laced with bits of burnt curry with such pleasure and think of it as just reward for all the hard work we had to do. What was once, in my earlier life, considered unfit for consumption by respectable people had now become a prized addition on the plates of those privileged few who happened to be the cooks for the day!

Later in life I realized that what I experienced then taught me that it is good to be hungry once in a while so that one appreciates the food that is laid before us.

Dual Existence

From my very first experiences in this boarding school, I began to realize that the residents in the hostel were leading two different lives: one as students of a fine school from 9 in the morning to 3 in the afternoon and the other as menial labourers, cooks and housekeepers in the hostel.

Our day began at daybreak but for the cooks even earlier because they had to prepare tea for the girls of their respective Houses and also start cooking lunch. After the plain cup of tea we had to go to the school building to do our homework, the cooks included. What little time was left after study hour was spent in having hurried baths; lunch would be served by 8:30 and we had to reach school by 9 sharp. There would be a short prayer service in the school chapel every day and after that the day's activities would begin. After two periods, there was a break of 15 minutes for physical exercise. After the 4th period we were allowed to go to the hostel for some measly snacks like a puny banana and a dry rusk while the day scholars had their tiffin in the school compound. There would be three more classes after the recess and at 3 pm the school would close.

For the hostellers, the task after school was to sweep the entire hostel compound to rid it of fallen leaves and other debris. The most hated part of this chore was pulling out the tough weeds called 'bon guti' in Assamese during the summer months. It is a plant with sticky seeds on long stems and which get stuck on clothes and are very difficult to remove. We had to pull out this tenacious weed with our bare hands and often its smooth but sharp stalks cut into our palms. In the intense heat of the afternoon this job was the most hated one among the chores we had to perform after school. We got nothing, not even a cup of tea between school-break and dinner which was served at 5 pm.

There was another study-hour from 6 to 7 in the evening when we had to go to the school to study and do our homework which would be plenty for each subject. The worst used to be arithmetic where we had to solve sums which were chosen by the teacher often outside the text book, sometimes up to ten or twelve, depending on her whim. There would be assignments for drawing maps of the various continents according to the scale specifications given by the geography teacher. No tracing was allowed and in spite of the need to correct our drawing by hand using a pencil and eraser, our note books had to be clean. Marks were deducted for presenting dirty work.

Lights-out was strictly at 8 pm, after which not even a squeak must be heard in the darkened hostel compound. The Matron, sometimes accompanied by the Superintendent would make a round of the Houses. There was a chowkidar who would come only after 8 and he would disappear before the hostellers awoke. Males of any rank, age or class were viewed with utmost suspicion and were 'suffered' only when absolutely necessary, like a night chowkidar for around a hundred girls in the hostel or the odd plumber or electrician who was allowed to come and do his job only during the time when the girls were at school.

There used to be a wall clock in the 4th House where the Matron had a room to herself. At 8 o'clock the Mahi of the House had to ring a brass bell hung in the front room to announce lights-out. When I became the Mahi of this House, I often used to put the hands of the clock back by 5 minutes so that we had extra time to finish whatever homework we were struggling with.

Once during a final examination, I managed to hoodwink the Matron by opening up an umbrella over a candle inside an empty biscuit tin and spreading a dark coloured cloth over the umbrella to catch up on some last- minute reading for the next day's exam which was Elementary Science. But the attempt lasted only for half an hour or so because my head started reeling, being cooped up inside the umbrella and so close to the fumes of the burning candle!

Taste of Failure

My first year in school was a total disaster. It was difficult to cope with the duties in the hostel and the amount of homework I had to finish in between the hostel chores every single day. If I slipped up in either, there would be the dreaded 'punishment'.

Matters were worse in the class. I was still struggling with the English alphabets, the capital and small letters proving the most difficult while my classmates were way ahead. I did slightly better in the other subjects which were taught in Assamese. Luckily for me my arithmetic was quite sound and I felt happy only during that class. The final exams arrived and I struggled to write the answers in all the subjects as best as I could and hoped that I would somehow pass. We waited eagerly for the day when the results would be announced.

Then the much anticipated day came and all the students were assembled in the big school chapel. We were seated on the rough jute carpet while the teachers and the Principal sat on the raised platform. On a table in front of the rows of chairs was a huge register which contained the names of all the students. After the preliminary address by the Principal, she began to read out the names of the successful students. It appeared that most of the students passed. As the names were announced in a descending order starting from class IX, I had to wait for a long time to hear my name, our class being the last. After the announcements for class V, I became more agitated but was still hopeful that I would pass. So far in my life, 'not passing' had never been a factor. I was a good student and had even earned a scholarship in the class III Board exam. So I remained hopeful until I realized that the Principal was closing the big register and my name had not been announced among those who were being promoted to the next class. I thought it was the most shameful thing that could ever happen to me. Not pass? I could not accept that.

I stood up where I had been sitting patiently and began to shout 'I have passed' and started to howl loudly. Every one was trying to get out of the chapel and when I saw that, I too followed them but still crying and screaming 'I have passed, I have passed'. I howled all the way to the hostel. The senior girls in my House tried to comfort me but I wouldn't give up. I kept on shouting that I had passed, and why was my name not announced? Because of the extreme agitation, I started to choke on my sobs and I was beginning to feel weak. Yet, I did not give up. My hoarse cry had turned to intermittent sobs but I would not listen to anyone. I kept repeating, 'I have passed, I have passed.' When I regained my strength and was starting to sob loudly again, I saw the Principal coming towards me and moments later she gathered me in her arms and told me that I had indeed 'passed' in the sense that all the teachers had agreed that I should be sent to class V because during the short time I was in class IV, I had been diligent and shown improvement in many subjects. The only reason she did not announce my name was that I could not be put in any kind of ranking in the class. This information somehow calmed me but I was still smarting from the fact that my name was not announced in public along with the names of those who had passed. I still could not understand why the Principal did not make this announcement in the chapel and began to feel angry. I wanted to protest about this but the presence of the Principal daunted me. Besides, my earlier hysterical outburst had exhausted me and so without a word I went to my bed and fell asleep immediately.

My academic career in this school started on this rather melodramatic note where the minimum pass marks were 60% in every subject. What this experience did for me was to instil a dreadful fear in my mind about 'failing'. From that early age, I resolved that I would be the best student in my class and secure the first position always. How little did I know what I would have to face in my quest for this position and how much I would have to struggle to achieve this in the senior classes!

1st and 2nd

The near disaster of being kept back in class IV taught me a new and valuable lesson. I may have been young but ever since my parents' death and the subsequent hardships that we had to endure before I was sent to this boarding school, had made me acutely aware of the harsh realities of life.

And here I was, already suffering from a greater sense of deprivation and even of abandonment to find myself in a situation where I seemed to have nobody to call my own. Added to that was the realization that I was way behind my classmates in studies too. But I was absolutely determined to do well in studies because I believed that it was the only way left for me to become somebody. I also assumed that I could beat all my classmates and achieve the first position in our class. Though I felt inferior to those girls with families, fine clothes and the attention they received from the teachers as well as the Super, my success in studies would somehow make me equal to them.

My fond hopes were however not to be realized so easily. When Class V started, we were all taken aback by the arrival of a much older girl in our class who, we were told, was a child widow! She was married off when she was six or seven and had to stay with her parents until she attained puberty according to the custom in their community. Only then would she be sent to her husband's home. But before this happened, her child-groom died and she found herself a widow without ever having had any contact with her husband. She became a figure of mystery and curiosity for all. But for me she turned out to be the obstacle in my pursuit of the first position in class.

Obviously her father was a very progressive man because he had kept a tutor for her at home to continue her studies while waiting to go to her husband's home and it continued after she became a child-widow. She was a bright student and managed the lower classes quite easily. But to appear in the board examination in class VI she had to attend regular classes from class V. That is why she took admission in class V with us. She was much older than most of us and did not mix very much with the classmates. But from the very beginning it became clear who would secure the first position in our class. At every examination result day when the report cards were distributed according to rank beginning with the first, I saw my dream of obtaining that first position go up in smoke and I used to shed tears even though I stood second in the class. The other classmates were puzzled at my behaviour and thought that I was making a ridiculous fuss. But this girl seemed to understand the reason for my grief though she did not say anything to anyone.

When our progress cards were distributed after the second term exams, I cried again because once again I was in the second position. She came to me during the games break and took me aside and said, "Look, when I pass the board exam, I'll move on to an Assamese medium high school because my father wants me to become a teacher in our village school which he is building. So don't be sad, when I leave, the first position will be yours because I know you are bright. Not only that, I see a strong determination in you to excel in whatever you do. Never give that up." When I heard these words coming from a person who was regarded by all of us as someone special, but who according to me was my rival also, I was stunned. But at the same time my spirits lifted and I stopped crying because her words showed that she understood my inner struggle. This fact reassured me somehow and gave me new hope. And it gave me new courage to live within that hope, thinking that if a clever and brave girl like her saw my potential, then sooner or later I would achieve my goal.

After more than half a century when I recall this particular episode, I begin to see how it must have been for her in a society which condemns widows, child or adult. And what must it have been like to defy social sanctions to continue with studies which were considered pointless for girls in most families, let alone a child widow. In fact we were told that when it became known that she was going to be admitted in our school, there was strong opposition not only from her in-laws but also from her own community. At that time we assumed that it was on account of our school being a Christian Missionary school but then we were a bit puzzled also because there were many Hindu girls in our school. In fact at least five of my classmates were Hindus and came from prominent families of the town. We were too young and naive then and did not understand that the opposition was based on more fundamental reasons because of the fact that this girl was a widow. But the child widow was supported by her father, who was prepared to face all opposition in order to bring enlightenment to just such a society. I do not know how authentic it is but we heard a rumour that in the beginning this girl was pelted with stones when she walked to school and for quite sometime her father used to escort her to school and back home. Gradually the furore died down and she walked to school like all the other day scholars without any incident. As I write this, I regret that I could not keep track of this remarkable woman and her achievements.

I only hope that she went on to fulfil the grand design her father had for her and that their efforts enlightened and benefited a society so immersed in the bonds of the past; also that she found some measure of fulfilment in her life.

Piss Bucket Disposers

I am quite certain that the immediate reaction to the topic of this section will be, 'What?' We are living in an age where through new knowledge and modern technology disposal of body waste has progressed to almost an art form and an expensive one at that. The toilet or washroom or whatever euphemism is applied to this section of the home has now become the most important facility in any building. When so much attention is lavished on this facility not only in homes, but posh hotels and even in public places, what is being described here may sound extremely crude and unbelievable. But it needs to be recorded because as hostellers we endured this horrible experience until our last year there and I wonder for how many more years the practice continued after we left.

The routine was to place a rusty iron bucket in front of every House in the evening for the girls to use at night. The reason was that the toilets being at a distance, almost at the perimeter fence, it would be dangerous for the girls to trudge there in the dark. The additional bogey was that unwanted elements may be lurking there to frighten or even kidnap the helpless girls! There was some merit in the latter argument because on several occasions miscreants had managed to enter the hostel at night and frightened the girls with their antics. So the buckets were placed in front of the Houses for the convenience of the girls. That is where you did 'it' at night and by morning on many days it would be brimming with the night's flow.

It was the juniors in the hostel who had to perform the hateful task of transporting the piss buckets to the Houses at dusk and carry the full buckets in the morning to the toilets. In order to reach the row of latrines we had to negotiate first, a downward slope and then an upward climb with the brimming buckets. Sometimes the contents would spill on to our frocks and we would stink the whole day if we did not get a chance to bathe and change before school. The buckets had to be rinsed with water and hung upside down on posts meant exclusively for the purpose. Even in this job one ran the risk of being 'punished' if the piss got spilled on the way or the buckets were not rinsed properly. The buckets had to be replaced quite often as they rusted and became corroded in no time at all. Also, in front of each House there was a permanent barren patch where the buckets stood at night and often overflowed.

Even half a century later as I write this, I cringe when I recall how much we hated this practice in the hostel. Of all the menial jobs we had to perform as hostellers, this stands out in my memory as one of the two most demeaning and hateful of them all.

Cowdung Collectors

The other task which the junior girls had to perform was to collect fresh cowdung from nearby sheds early in the mornings. Saturday was a holiday and it was on this day when we had to give each House a thorough cleaning by taking out not only our bed linen but also our beds, boxes and stools and putting them out in the open. Apart from airing our clothes and dusting the furniture, the most important reason for doing this was to plaster the constantly cracking mud floors with a mixture of fresh cow dung and soil. And it was the job of a pair of juniors to go and collect the dung from a shed belonging to the hostel chowkidar very early on Saturday morning and on some occasions from neighbouring sheds too.

Only fresh dung would serve the purpose, therefore you had to beat the girls from the other Houses in reaching the shed first; otherwise you had to go from shed to shed in the neighbourhood begging for some fresh dung. These early morning expeditions in search of fresh cowdung have stayed in my mind like a scary dream where you heard weird and frightening sounds of night creatures, the mournful lowing of cows tethered in the ramshackle sheds and sometimes, the silhouettes of trees resembling ghostly figures would send chills of terror into our young hearts. These spectres always seemed to be watching our pathetic scrambles for this much needed ingredient to spruce up the mud floors of the various Houses.

If it was loathsome in summer, it was worse in winter. We had to get up while it was still pitch-dark and start on our foray. Venturing out of the fence of the hostel, sometimes we would be startled by the indignant hoot of an owl shattering the eerie silence. On certain mornings the last lingering light of the fading moon added its own horror to the surreal atmosphere. And walking barefoot on dew-drenched grass would shoot the winter cold right into our fear-filled hearts. But we had to collect the precious shit; so virtually taking our lives in our hands we would finish our errand and hurry back to our respective Houses. After the mud plastering on the floor dried, all the things had to be brought inside once again and then at this juncture another form of torture awaited the juniors. It was here that the seniors always bullied and made the juniors their errand girls. We survived this weekly exercise, however tiring and trying because we had something special to look forward to: on Saturdays we got a special dinner: chana dal, roti and some real meat for our dinner! It was indeed something to look forward to after a hectic day's labour.

Hiuen Tsang

When I was assigned to a regular House after about a week of my arrival, I was 'appropriated' by some seniors who were already in class X. As a result, I had to perform all kinds of errands for them, like fetching water for them, carrying books and messages to their friends. And sometimes they would make me run to the furthest House saying that someone wanted me there, only to laugh when I came back and reported that no one there had asked for me. Saturdays were the worst. Apart from washing and airing my own clothes and things, I had to take care of the needs of these seniors. Not satisfied with torturing me with these chores they would make fun of my appearance calling me Hiuen Tsang because of my Mongolian features and the fact that my hair was cut with a short fringe falling over my forehead.

To add to my humiliation, they began to make fun of my metal bowl and plate too, (kahi and bati, in Assamese) which I had carried from home as instructed by the hostel authorities. Every hosteller had to bring a plate and cup for her use.

The ragging continued for quite some time and I had to endure it because I was in the junior most class and had to do the bidding of the seniors. But things came to a head one Saturday and I seemed to have lost it. Being unable to take their harassment and taunting anymore, I hurled the 'bati' on the wall which broke into two pieces. The senior girls stopped in mid-laughter and fell silent. Encouraged by their shocked faces, I ripped the frock I was wearing down the middle shouting, 'You all are fit only to be step-mothers!' and with the torn frock flapping on my naked front, I ran out.

The senior girls gave chase and after making them huff and puff after me round the big compound several times, I came back to the House quite exhausted. When the tired girls reached the House, they pleaded and coaxed me to take off my torn frock and one senior hurriedly took out her sewing kit, mended the frock frantically and made me wear it again before anyone could report the matter to the Matron.

From that day onwards I was left alone and the seniors treated me with some amount of grudging respect. That was perhaps the first incident in my life which taught me that the best way to cope with bullies is to stand up to them.

But I still bear the scar from another incident from that period of my 'apprentice-ship'. I was ordered by one particularly aggressive senior to draw water from the hand-pump and carry two buckets to the bathroom so that she could have a leisurely bath. I proceeded to do her bidding. The iron buckets were heavy and when filled with water, it became difficult for me to carry it to the bath-house by myself. But somehow the first bucket was safely deposited in one of the cubicles of the bath-house. By the time I filled the second bucket and tried to lift it I was exhausted but I had to deposit it somehow in the cubicle. So I tried to half-drag and half-carry it; in the process some of the water had spilled and I finally managed to reach my destination with only half a bucket of water. But when I entered the cubicle, I slipped on a patch of melted soap and my right shin was caught in the rusty, jagged end of the corrugated tin partition between the cubicles. There was a searing pain and I screamed and screamed. The senior girls heard my scream and came rushing to the bath-house to investigate. When they saw my state, one of them picked me up to take me to the hostel infirmary. But the girl whose errand I was performing managed to warn me not to say anything to the Matron about her role in the accident. When the nurse asked me what happened I sobbed and timidly replied, 'I slipped in the bathroom'. Luckily for me it was only a flesh wound but it was an ugly gash and took almost two weeks to even begin healing. It did heal eventually but to this day I bear the scar on my right shin.

Sundays

Being a Mission school, Sundays were of course devoted solely to church-going and attending prayer meetings in the respective Houses in the evening. We used to be 'escorted' to church, which was at a walking distance from our hostel, by the Principal and Superintendent accompanied by the Matron and those teachers who lived on the school campus.

It was a ceremony of sorts: we would stand in a long line of twos, all wearing white saris and frocks and would be bare footed. We were not allowed to wear coloured dresses to church and of course shoes were a prohibited item from our lives, either in school, church or hostel.

The church services were uninspiring and tedious; the only good thing I liked about these outings was that they *were* outings of some kind and we got the chance to sing as a congregation. Collection time was always tricky, sometimes we could spare a small coin for the plate from our pocket money but more were the occasions when we turned our heads away in embarrassment on account of not being able to do so.

During my first year in the hostel, the little pocket money I was given was all spent in buying pencil, rubber, paper for doing rough work as well as soap, hair oil and a post-card or two. There were many Sundays when I could not put even a small coin on the offering plate. So I went to the Superintendent who used to give me Rs.2 and 8 annas every month as pocket money and requested her to increase the amount a bit so that I could put some coins on the offering plate on Sundays. I also told her that I felt ashamed of not being able to do that because the amount I got was not enough. She looked at me for a long time without saying anything. In the end, she said to me, "Do not be ashamed, God knows why you cannot offer anything." My pocket money remained the same for another two years.

Some Sundays the hostellers would be taken for walks around our neighbourhood. Here also we had to walk in twos and I remember that we were seldom taken through inhabited areas; rather our route often lay through empty spaces with very little vegetation and even if we met people we knew, we were not allowed to speak to anyone. These walks were like exchanging one kind of boredom for another but I learned to like them because it was a kind of freedom which took us out of the hostel boundaries and I also found that the walks gave me more time to think about all sorts of things.

Letters

In our hostel, there was a peculiar postal facility: we could write and receive letters but with certain conditions. Before posting, our letters had to be deposited in a special basket in the Super's office, un-sealed. She and the Matron would first read all the letters and then they would decide which could be posted right away and which ones had to be 'discussed' with the writers, often returned with the admonition to write 'better' letters; meaning that we were not to send any complaints to our parents and guardians or mention anything negative about the school. The other condition was that we could write only to authorized persons like parents and guardians; to write to our siblings also we had to have prior permission from our guardians. When letters came for the girls, they were opened and read by the Super and the Matron first, before being distributed to the recipients after school.

Receiving a letter was the most exciting moment for the lucky recipient; it was the moment that every hostel girl lived for. There would be rejoicing all around, the letters would be read and re-read and every word treasured as if it was a hug from loved ones bringing some joy into an otherwise gruelling and mirthless existence. Those who did not receive any letter would mope around for a while but the pressure of chores awaiting us would not give us much time to sulk and we would once again settle to our routine, forgetting the momentary disappointment and sorrow.

But for someone like me this daily disappointment became a cruel fact of life. If I received anything it would

be a postcard from one of my brothers once or twice a year.
I knew that I did not have anybody except them to write to
me but it did not prevent me from hoping every afternoon
that somewhere among the pile of letters in the Super's hand
there would be one for me. The daily hurt grew to become
a huge pain in my heart making me realize how alone I was
in this world. I felt abandoned and outraged at the same
time; thinking that there was nobody in this wide world to
acknowledge my existence. How I longed for even a scrap of
paper with my name on it to tell me that I was remembered,
that somebody cared. I felt truly wretched and impoverished
in those bitter moments. Material poverty, one learned to
cope with but emotional impoverishment of this kind creates
a big void in one's heart which remains for life.

It is not as if I did not receive any letters at all; I did
receive some but it was only after I went to high school.
However, the joy of those rare moments could not in any way
mitigate the regular disappointments of not receiving letters
as frequently as did the other girls. But even this brief elation
after a long gap was marred by the receipt of a postcard from
some one whose name was not on the authorized list.

During my second year in high school, one afternoon I
joined the group of hopefuls as always and waited patiently
until there was only one post-card in the Super's hand. By
now the happy recipients were skipping away to the hostel
with their precious letters followed dejectedly by the losers
of the day. I made as if to follow them when the Super
called out my name and gestured towards me to follow her
into her cluttered office. I obeyed and as soon as we were
alone she showed me the name of the sender on the card
and demanded, "Who is he?" I looked at the name and could
not place him immediately and replied, "I don't know." She
raised her voice and asked me again, "Who is he? If you do
not know him why is he writing to you?" I looked again and

suddenly it occurred to me that it could be the name of one of my elder brother's friends. I replied, "I remember now, he is my brother's friend." She insisted, "Why is he writing to you? Is he your boy friend?" At this insinuation all my pent-up frustration and anger flared up and I literally shouted back at her, "No he is not my boy friend and you can keep the letter." Saying this I ran all the way to the hostel, crying.

From that day onwards I did not bother to wait with the others for the letter- distribution ritual and whatever precious few I received were brought to me by my friends.

Piano Lessons

During the entire period of my stay in the school, one phase remains in my memory as the happiest: it began from the day I was allowed to receive piano lessons. I think I was in class VI. But it was not an easy entrance to this 'elite' group and it happened mainly because of my sheer tenacity.

There were two pianos in our school: one in the bungalow where the Principal and Superintendent lived and one in the school chapel. While the former was out of bounds for students, the one in the chapel could be used by students who were learning the instrument. Among the students were the daughter of a tribal missionary, the daughter of a tea planter and daughters of some alumni of the school. They were mostly high school students and were treated by all as members of an exclusive club. On certain important days, the senior students took turns to accompany the hymn singing and on a special occasion when some foreign visitors were present, two of them presented solo recitals. I looked at these girls with awe and admiration and resolved that one day I too would be like them. I found out that to be enrolled in the class one had to be tested by the teacher, who was the wife of the missionary of the region residing in the town.

She, we were told, was a reputed pianist, having won second prize in a national contest in America. She was also soft spoken and beautiful.

I was still in the sixth class but I wanted to learn the instrument so badly that on a Saturday when she came to assess her students' progress, I went and told her that I also wanted to enrol in her class. She looked at me and wanted me to spread my hands. I did and saw what she also saw: my knobby fingers roughened by scrubbing dishes and doing other menial jobs. Still she asked me to cover the keys starting from the middle C to as far my little finger could stretch. I could barely manage up to the next C: just one octave. She shook her head sadly and said that my reach was not good enough and that my hands were far too rough. She could not take me in. I broke into tears and ran out.

But I did not give up: I tried pulling my fingers wide to increase the span and washed my hands several times a day. Three Saturdays later I was there again. The lady gave me a wry smile and called me in. Once again she asked me to show her my hand span. I stretched out my hands and opened my palms. I do not know what I expected and unless there was a miracle, my hands would remain the same as the first time. She looked into my eyes and perhaps saw the desperation and hunger for music, I will never know. But she gave my hands a gentle squeeze and said that I could join the beginners' class. I was ecstatic and felt like I had won a big prize!

I started learning the scales, then the simple chords and after a month she taught me how to read the notes on both the clefs. My right hand was doing fine on the keyboard but the left hand refused to move at the same pace as the right. The flats and sharps were another hurdle. However, the piano practice sessions became the most peaceful and soothing moments of my day and I was beginning to experience a sense of belonging somewhere.

The teacher was most encouraging. After I played the scales and simple pieces assigned by her the previous Saturday she would pat me on the head and say that she would play for me some original compositions as a reward. They were intricate and beautiful pieces and I would feel transported to another planet! We were introduced to some basic work books on piano practice, two of which I remember are John Thomson's *Modern Course for the Piano* and another by someone called John W. Shaum. I made steady progress and when I eventually graduated to playing simplified versions from famous composers like Chopin, Schubert and Mozart, she would again play the original pieces asking me to observe her hands. There were many occasions when she was so engrossed in performing the original from memory that she forgot my presence there. Then suddenly she would give a small laugh and try to apologise to me but for such momentary exclusions of course, I only felt highly privileged. These happy diversions only whetted my appetite and strengthened my resolve to become a good piano player like her and I felt that something special had come my way at last.

Among the hostellers also, the piano students were perceived to be a privileged lot. I especially remember an occasion when we were invited by our piano teacher to her bungalow and she gave us tea with huge slices of what she called Angel's Frost Cake! She also showed us a packet which contained the ingredients for a Devil's Cake. She explained that while the cake we ate was white and called Angel's Cake, the other one would be almost black because it had chocolate. We could not talk of anything else for weeks except the heavenly taste of the cake we had eaten and this made many of the girls envious of us.

I was diligent with my piano practice and my teacher was amazed how, after persistent efforts, I was able to extend my reach at least one key beyond the octave! She took a special liking to me and we became friends. She also told me that on a previous Saturday, her husband had come to pick her up while we were still practising. I still remember it was a piece called *Le Arabesque* or something like that which had many staccato beats. It was lively and I was having a really good time playing it. It seems her husband thought it was her on the keyboard. But when she told him it was her student, he told her that he considered her time was well-spent with such a student. I understood what he meant and was overjoyed.

As the other students were also making good progress, our teacher began planning for a concert for the school. While she chose the pieces for the others, she informed me that she would play a duet with me, her on the treble clef and I on the bass, in the next school function to be held a month later. We started practicing; but unfortunately for us, fate intervened; her husband had contracted malaria as a result of many evangelistic trips to interior villages and after a particularly virulent attack he died. The funeral service was held in the local church. There were many mourners including the hostellers. Many non-Christians who had come into contact with the dedicated missionary in his work among the poor and sick people flocked to the ceremony from nearby villages. The outpouring of grief was spontaneous as he was genuinely loved by the people whom he served not only as a missionary but also as a friend. The people wept openly and I remember how the hostellers also cried as if someone very close had died.

Soon after his death, the family had to leave Assam and it meant that our piano lessons would also come to an end. My curious love affair with the piano was thus cut short by fate, but I still recall the gentle and understanding lady who gave me a chance to enter the world of music and get acquainted, no matter how briefly and superficiously, with some of the most delightful composers of all time. After that phase of my life ended so abruptly, I never got another opportunity to continue with my lessons and today I can just about locate the middle C on the keyboard!

Another episode is associated with piano lessons but it has nothing to do with music. We in the piano class were allowed half an hour's practice time every day after study hours in the morning and for me it was the most beautiful time of the day. Sometime during one of my depressing moments I had shot off a six-page letter to my brother letting off all my pent-up frustrations and most probably writing some crazy things as well. I had to deposit it in an open envelope in the Super's basket as was the rule so that she could read it before posting it.

What I had written must have troubled her because I later learnt that she showed it to the Matron, as well as the Principal. She called me to her room after school and asked me why I had written such a letter. I did not say anything. I just stood there like a statue without even looking at her. After about ten minutes she let me go to the hostel. But the next day she came to the chapel where I was practicing scales on the piano. I told her that I had to finish my practice because the next day was Saturday when the piano teacher would come to check on us. She went outside without saying anything.

After I finished my practice I tip-toed to the door and saw her waiting for me on the porch. I quickly turned inside and through a side door slipped out of the chapel and walked to the hostel through a narrow path which joined the school and hostel boundaries. She never mentioned the letter again but I am sure that it was never posted.

Bloody Rags

Towards the end of my sixth class, the inevitable happened.
I began menstruating. I did not know what to do. I managed
the first day somehow though my panty got thoroughly
soaked and some spots appeared on my frock. One of my
classmates observed me sneaking towards the bathrooms and
followed me. She was the one whom I always helped with
arithmetic; she was also a year older and was 'experienced' in
these matters. When I saw her I stood facing her and glared
at her. She came to me and said, "Don't worry, I know what's
happened, it happens to everybody, there is nothing to be
ashamed of." She asked me if I had any rags, I said no. Telling
me to wait for her, she ran to her House and came back with
a few. Then taking a string she showed me how to strap it
round my waist with the rag folded like baby's napkin to be
draped between my legs. She also said that I had to wash the
bloody rags every day so that I would have some clean ones to
change into. She even taught me how to wash these rags. First
one had to pound on the bloody part with a stone and pour
lots of water in order to wash out all the blood; then use soap
to wash it clean. With soap being such a precious commodity
which I had to buy with my meagre pocket money, it was an
invaluable lesson in making a cake of soap go a long way.

I was clumsy with the rags in the beginning but eventually
learnt the trick. And so every month there would be these
four or five days of bloody rags and discomfort. The extra
time needed to change and wash these rags had somehow
to be fitted into the impossible schedule of school tasks and
hostel chores, but I had to manage and after a month or two,
this particular exercise became a part of my usual routine.

Entry into this stage however did not do anything to
dampen my exuberance at games and sports until the day
near-disaster struck. There was a basket-ball match between

our class and the VIIth class during the mid-day break and I was bouncing away with the ball to the basket when I stumbled and fell. I heard a loud snap and knew that my rag-string had come undone! If I stood up the whole bloody bundle would fall off, so I pretended to be hurt and when my classmate came near me I whispered in her ears about what happened. She immediately took charge; she twisted my skirt round my legs and virtually carried me towards the toilets where she helped me to re-do the string.

The taboo regarding menstrual blood may be interpreted differently by different people but the greatest fear in my mind when thus faced with public exposure of my state was my inability to protect my secret selfhood. It was one thing for others to know that I had attained puberty but it was quite another matter to be humiliated publicly with the proof in this vulgar manner. When my bloody rag was once again secured in place, I felt as if I was saved from some form of death. I know that I could have never lived down that public humiliation but for the presence of mind of my friend. And even today when I am at last freed from the monthly 'curse', I remember my friend with gratitude.

There are many people to whom I am indebted for their kindness towards me during the most difficult moments in my life but this friend of mine is special and to say that I am merely 'grateful' to her would be to demean the essence of her understanding of my predicament and protecting me from 'shame' at the most crucial juncture of my transition from being a girl and entering that rarefied domain of being a woman. Wherever you are Jean, God bless you.

End of Junior School

Class VI was a crucial year for every student. In order to enter High School, one had to pass a Board Examination. For this examination there was a regulation that every girl had to submit a work-book where we had to enter specimens of all the different kinds of stitches, miniature frocks and panties and most important of all, a proper Assamese 'mekhela' (sarong) woven by ourselves at the school looms! Anyone who did not or could not submit this on time would not be allowed to sit for the main examination. I managed all the other requirements in our sewing classes but the mekhela was proving to be a colossal hurdle for me. The weaving was supervised by a lady who belonged to our church. She would come during study hours in the morning and give instructions to all of us. The older girls in our class took no time at all to finish their mekhelas because most of them had already learnt the craft from their mothers and aunts at home as the mekhela was the native dress of Assamese women and every girl was required to learn the skill. I was the only one who had never seen a loom before coming to this school and now I had to accomplish what seemed to be an impossible task. Time was running out for me and even the kind lady seemed to have given up on me. Every session at the loom was crying time for me. I would try to pass the shuttle between the layers of thin thread and the result would be a loud twang snapping several strands. Joining the threads again was beyond me and the instructor would shake her head and making sure that the Super or Matron could not see her she would take my place and weave a few inches on the pretext of showing me how to join the torn threads. Towards the end of term, I was the only one in that miserable weaving room trying to produce a mekhela for the Board exam.

I do not know how it was done but just two days before the deadline the mekhela was declared finished, cut from its frame and, folded in such a way as to hide the numerous knots and gaps where I had snapped the vital threads. It was added to my work-book and dispatched to the authorities.

This near fiasco did not teach me any skill on the loom nor did I attempt anything so complicated in later life. About this particular experience, I have only a vague impression that I did assist someone in weaving a mekhela in my sixth class though I never learned what marks I got for my craft work. But I passed the Board examination in the 1st division and won another scholarship!

De-lousing Queues and De-worming Days

Having lice in your head was a matter of shame for you and concern for the authorities in school because lice have a fantastic way of finding new lodgings very quickly. This was a sore point with me because with my very thick hair, no matter how short, lice did find me an excellent host. I remember one incident when they had to shave off my hair as there was no other way of getting rid of the crawling pests! That was before I came to the hostel. Even here the hateful creatures somehow got to my hair and merrily multiplied. For such as me, there would be a delousing queue on the infirmary steps every morning after study-hour when girls with lice were expected to de-louse each other by standing in a line where you had to look for lice on the head of the one in front while the one behind did the same for you. At the end of the week, the hostel nurse would inspect each head and certify whether or not one had to continue with the process. As far as I remember I became a permanent member of that queue for a long time even during my high school days!

Every term a Saturday would be chosen to administer doses of castor oil to the girls for the purpose of de-worming. We used to dread these Saturdays because we hated the taste of castor oil and many girls used to vomit it out the first few times. But the experienced nurse had a fool-proof method of forcing it down the throat. She would pour the dose into the mouth and quickly grab your nose and clamp on your mouth so that you had no alternative but to swallow the foul liquid. Since there seemed to be no escape from this ordeal, we learnt to tolerate the taste and the Saturdays seemed to pass without any hassle. But then one day it was announced that we would be inoculated against something or the other on the coming Saturday and many girls began howling even before the day arrived. There was complete chaos on the day itself. Many girls started running here and there looking for hiding places. But the infirmary had only three rooms and most of the panicky girls were prized out of corners and held by the Matron while the nurse administered the injection, amid shrill cries. When the melee was over, it was discovered from the register that one girl from our House was missing. After a frantic search, she was discovered crouching on top of the big medicine cabinet inside the infirmary. How and when she climbed up there was a mystery because she was big-built. She put up a brave fight by screaming and yelling but was eventually urged down from her perch and the nurse happily pushed the needle into her quavering muscles accompanied by her hysterical screams. But the job was done and the inoculated girls walked to their Houses complaining loudly of the pain.

Rumours

Life in the hostel was virtually insulated from the outside world. But there was an amazing network which would time and again spread the wildest rumours. Some were just that: wild rumours but a few turned out to be based on some truth. One such rumour was about the chowkidar's daughter named Miriam. I do not remember how I came to hear about it but it was whispered that the girl was pregnant. We did not know her properly because she was not allowed in the hostel grounds. But from the glimpses we had of her it appeared that she was very small in stature though she was supposed to be around fifteen or so. The senior girls in our House would clam up whenever the juniors were around. But when they thought that we were out of earshot, they spoke in loud whispers and giggled. It was said that Miriam's mother died while giving birth to her brother who did not survive his first year. So she was living with her father in the small shack just outside our compound from where we collected cowdung on Saturdays. That she was pregnant without being married was scandalous enough but what was more shocking was the fact that people were saying that it was her father who might have made her this way. After these details became known, it was no longer a rumour; it became a topic of grave discussions, especially among the senior girls. We began to talk about him like he was the devil himself and shuddered to think what he might do when we went to his cowshed so early in the morning on Saturdays to collect fresh cowdung.

Things came to such a pass that the girls began to say openly that they would never go to his cowshed, whatever be the consequence. The agitation of the girls soon reached the Matron because some girls, who were close to the Matron, carried the tale to her. She in turn, reported to the Super what was being said in the hostel.

It was a grave situation and the girls' talk must have caused additional worry for the school authorities. They did not want news of this scandal to reach the parents and guardians of the girls. They had to take a swift decision. A few days later, we came to know that we had a new chowkidar and every one heaved a sigh of relief. The Saturday excursions for collecting fresh cowdung would continue as usual, though there would be no Miriam or her father in the cottage.

The girls soon stopped talking about this scandal but I thought about Miriam and her baby for a long time, wondering where they went and what might have happened to them.

Football Team

Apart from the fifteen minute breaks for games from Monday to Friday in school, we had no other sports activities in the hostel. One Saturday afternoon as I gloomily lolled on the sprawling grounds of the hostel I began to think how in this wide open space we could play so many games. But which game and with what? Then suddenly I remembered kicking my brothers' football around the house when they were away. That's it, I thought but where would I get a football? I toyed with the idea for a few days and decided that if a real football could not be had, I would make one! I would collect paper, old clothes, even twigs and string, anything that could be shredded and moulded and I would create a football! It took me more than a week to wheedle these materials from my mates as well as the seniors and start on the often frustrating work. I had to work fast before the Matron discovered the rubbish and banned the whole idea itself. My industry paid off and one afternoon I introduced the odd-looking football to the girls and invited them to take part in the 'competition'!

I knew a few football terms, thanks to my brothers and their craze for the game and assumed the 'captaincy' of my team comprising of my class mates. Influenced by my enthusiasm, some others promptly joined up and became the other team.

So everyday after the mandatory labour of cleaning up the hostel surroundings and before dinner we began to have a football 'match', a highly exaggerated misnomer because between random kicks it was mostly shrill cries and wild dashes which indicated that there was some kind of game going on. In between shrieks, terms like foul, hand-ball and penalty would ring out though I suspect most of the girls did not have the faintest idea what they meant. The much awaited cry of 'goal' would resound once in a while but if that was against our team I would counter it by shouting 'offside' though I did not honestly know what it exactly meant and how it was determined that with this word the goal could be nullified.

What my play mates did not know was that I was as ignorant about the rules of the game as them and was merely repeating the vocabulary used by my brothers when they played. But even without any proper knowledge of how they were applied, I had the advantage because of the vocabulary. By creating a football out of nothing and organizing the few games, I was perhaps trying, not only to create a few exciting moments in a dull routine life, but was also trying to assume a leadership role among my peers.

But the one-sided domination and my ignorance of proper rules, as they soon found out put paid to my brief moments of glory in the arena and the teams got disbanded quietly. Before this happened, some of the girls had already withdrawn from the teams, saying that the Naga girls deliberately kicked them on the shin instead of on the ball. My room-mate summed it all up. "Anyway, the football was going out of shape and we were getting fed up with your kicks on our shins."

It was a good thing that we tried to play football during our last junior year when we were still wearing frocks because from the seventh class it was compulsory for us to wear saris or mekhela-sador only as we were now in High School.

It was also the year when I followed a group of seniors and got baptized in the dirty pond in front of the local church, not out of any conviction but because some of my friends were getting baptized. Thus I became a registered member of the church and could participate in the ritual of the Lord's Supper on the appointed days of every month.

In school however, we played games like basket ball, bean bag competition and a peculiar game called Captain Ball. In this game, as in every other game, there were two sides, the leaders of each team being called captains and hence perhaps the name. There were four circles in the field and each captain had to stand inside the east and west circles. She would be guarded by a fielder of the opposite side who had to stand outside the circle. In the same manner one player of each side had to stand inside the north and south circles likewise guarded. Four other fielders had to scramble for the ball and try to pass it on to her team-mate in the relevant circle. The players in the north and south circles would then try to throw it to their captains in the east or west circle who had to make a clean catch, without the opposite fielder touching the ball or she overstepping the circle line. If successful, the team would score 2 points for every clean catch. The fielders could not send the ball directly to their captains; they only had to feed it to their mates in the circles. The fielders had the toughest time as they had to cover a lot of ground to gain possession of the ball in an unlimited field.

All these years I have been trying to find out more about this game, whether it is an obscure American game introduced in our extra-curricular activities and if it was still played in America. When I went to America I asked about it but no one seemed to have heard of it or seen it played anywhere. Ignorance about this still persists, but when we played it we thoroughly enjoyed the sheer physicality involved in the process of pursuing the ball and I particularly enjoyed the fun-filled release of energy that left me quite exhausted after the game but also provided a sense of exhilaration after every win.

High School

Entering high school was like stepping into another world. There were so many changes that the world I inhabited for the last two years seemed to have disappeared. In high school, all the subjects henceforth would be taught in English and for the first time we could use pen and ink to write with. There would however be the language subjects or an alternative subject for those who were not able to cope with the literature papers in Assamese. Since I had studied in that medium up to class VI, I was considered proficient enough to be assigned to the literature group. The others would have to study the elementary papers up to class VIII. There would also be a new subject called Bible Study which every student had to take, irrespective of whatever religion one professed. But there was a redeeming clause: there would be only 'grading' in that subject and it would have no bearing on the overall marks of the student. It did however mean a lot of extra work because we had not only to memorize all the names of the sixty-six books of both the Old and New Testaments but also had to read the entire Bible beginning from the book of Genesis right up to Revelations. But that is not all: we started our Bible classes with having to sketch the creation story in all its seven stages! Though we knew that the final grades would not be counted for the results, we had to do our assignments in this subject too like in all the others.

And then there was a change in the dress code too: high school girls could no longer wear frocks; they had to wear either a sari or mekhela-sador to school, as well as to church. This change-over caused me a few initial worries and also some moments of embarrassment. I had never worn a sari or mekhela-sador in my life and managing the length of cloth was trying, to say the least. But I had to wear them instead of the comfortable frocks. My hair too was short and I still had a fringe and I must have cut a very sorry figure. Every one tittered when I entered the class on the first day of high school wearing a sari clumsily and sporting my 'Hiuen Tsang' hair cut! But that was not all. During our game break one day, we were playing a game called 'guddu', a game similar to 'kabbadi'. Muttering 'guddu' 'guddu', I ventured into the opposition's territory trying to touch some of them. I could not move fast enough on account of the mass of cloth in the sari. Trying to manage the awkward garment I tried to push on without being caught. But my tactics did not work as they would have if I was wearing a frock. And as I was not quick enough, some big girls grabbed me and tried to hold on to me. Unfortunately for them, they held on to my sari end, at which point I quickly unravelled the folds and escaped with just my petticoat! We won the point. In spite of these early mishaps, I eventually mastered the art of wearing a sari by the end of my stay in the school.

Study hours would also be different; high school students would have both morning and evening study hours. On Saturdays, we would have study hours without the supervision of teachers. The announcement was shocking at first because it was something completely out of character with the system of strict supervision that we had been subjected to so far, both in school and the hostel. When we were confronted with the first Saturday study hour of this nature, the Principal assembled us in the Chapel room and explained to us the rationale behind it. She said that through this system, we would learn how to be 'on our honour': to observe the rules of regular study hours and that meant that we were to be the monitors of our own actions during that period. She further added that by following this new rule, we were to prove that we were trustworthy, not only in the estimate of the teachers but of ours as well. Any discipline required for this period would have to be enforced by us on ourselves. No complaints would be entertained; we were free to study anything we wanted, including books from the small library which would be kept open for us every Saturday.

It was disconcerting at first, this new freedom, having no teachers with hawk-eyes to watch over our activities. Going to the library room itself daunted us at first because so far our movements were always strictly monitored and we had to seek permission even to move from our desks. But once we got used to the novelty of this unfamiliar freedom, we began to enjoy Saturday morning study hours. It was a brand new feeling to be all on our own. We also felt proud that we were trusted to do the correct thing by ourselves. It was as if we were given a new status as responsible adults.

I spent almost the entire 90 minutes browsing through the books in the library. There were books of many kinds, essays, journals, magazines and illustrated books on science and atlases. But what attracted me most were back issues of *Time*, *Life* and *The National Geographic* magazines. Reading these helped me immensely with the English language as well as expanding my horizon of knowledge in so many different ways. The big illustrated atlases intrigued me, making me realize how big the world was and how varied. They showed me the wonderful flora, fauna and other resources of the continents and gave fascinating facts about each. When I went to the sections illustrating the mineral resources of different countries, the precious and semi-precious stones captivated my imagination and made me weave fantastic dreams of owning some of them one day! And then the natural phenomena in the different continents, the very ones which we had to plot on the maps we drew so painstakingly for each one of them. Here in the atlas, they looked beautiful and alive! Within the small room the world I had known so far seemed to have expanded, and along with this sensation, my own self also seemed to have acquired a new dimension. The feeling was exhilarating and I was reluctant to leave it when the bell went off.

Those Saturday mornings gave me the comforting assurance that someone out there believed in us and was trying to instil in our young minds the value of moral integrity of the self. This not only bolstered my own self-confidence but also created a deep reverence for my Principal who was guiding us in our transition from adolescence to maturity, not only by preaching but by integrating the lesson into our practical routine. I have treasured this experience through which I learnt to cultivate self-discipline and nurture self-respect and to respect these qualities in others too. This has stood me in good stead all these years, as I believe it has, for every one who enjoyed this unique privilege in their high school years. Saturday study hour thus ceased to be a routine; it became our window to the immense world beyond, where if only one believed and persisted, everything was possible

The first two years of high school however, were disappointing as far as my dream of securing the 1st position in class was concerned. It was on account of my Assamese papers which were basically literature oriented where it was difficult to score beyond 75% to 80% at best. But on the other hand, here was my rival who could score above 90% in the basic vocabulary and grammar papers she was taking. She had added advantage because she was proficient in Bengali which is very similar to Assamese in terms of alphabets and much of the vocabulary. However this does not in any way detract any thing from her merit because she was a brilliant student and our competition was always very close. I could achieve this elusive goal only in my 9th class onwards because at this stage she had to take Commercial Geography papers and it was not possible for her to secure the kind of marks she got in the earlier language papers. I beat her easily and kept the first position until I passed the Matric examination in the 1st Division with Distinction in History. My so-called rival also passed the Matric exam in 1st Division with a Distinction in one of the subjects, I've now forgotten which. Also, I would like to add here that I did quite well in one of the Assamese papers securing 82%! but less in the other, so the aggregate of the two did not add up to 80%, therefore no Distinction there.

In High School we had to take a subject which was simply called Hygiene. In this subject our lessons started from the human anatomy which we had to draw showing the various systems like the Digestive, Respiratory, Nervous and Blood circulation systems. And then there were chapters on the various diseases etc. where at one stage we had to draw the different types of mosquitoes and which ones caused malaria. Another section dealt with the various nutrients for the body available in food sources. I am enumerating these because one important function of the body, the Reproductive System, was not taught till we were well into the second term in class X. For teaching this section, the school brought a Missionary Nursing Superintendent from Jorhat Mission Hospital. She was an American lady and her lessons were heavily laced with Biblical references. When it came to the actual process of human procreation, she said two things which have stayed in my mind all these years. About a child's birth, she began her lesson by saying this, "People say that miracles do not happen these days. But I would like to tell you that for me, every time a child is born, it is the greatest miracle that ever happens to man and this miracle continues to happen all over the world every day". At that time the true import of her words were not properly understood because the notion of a miracle was always linked in my mind to magic, even in the Biblical stories of the fish and loaves and Jesus walking on water etc.

The true meaning of her words was revealed to me only when my first child was born and I held the perfectly formed tiny human being in my arms. I was overwhelmed by the realization that I was somehow instrumental in the creation of another human being! It was only then that I understood what the teacher was referring to as a miracle; it was the human body itself which originates in another body and in turn becomes the agent for reproducing its own species. Therefore the human reproductive system, among all the systems in the body, was unique, its functioning was awe-inspiring and by highlighting this aspect, she was trying to instil in us the right perspective on the life process. We were however too young at that stage to understand the full import of her words and I am sure that like me in later life, my classmates also realized the true meaning of the word 'miracle' through their own experiences.

I also clearly remember the other thing she said by way of caution for young girls not to be misled by the flattery of boys whose only motive, she said, is to enjoy the pleasures of the female body. Condemning pre-marital sex as sin, she left us with this remark, "The boy can always get up and go away, but the girl has to bear the consequences and damnation for such an act".

Old *Time* Magazine Pages as Book Covers

Each year when we got our new texts and exercise books we were instructed to put covers on each. Sometimes we were given brown papers for this and when these ran out we were given old magazine pages instead to cover the books.

I do not exactly remember when it started but one year in high school we were given pages of old *Time* magazines to use as book covers. That was also the time when I had begun to read everything available as though propelled by an inner urge to devour every written word. When I discovered what was being distributed as book covers I went to every classmate begging them to let me read the words on their pages before they covered their books. Some were annoyed because this delayed their job but when they saw the intensity in my eyes, they let me read them. The random readings however left me totally dissatisfied because there was no continuity. Then I began to check the page numbers that each got and would once again go to them in sequence and plead with them to allow me to read the text again. Most of my classmates obliged but some did not and became quite hostile, even threatening to tell 'miss' about what I was doing. So I had to be content with whatever I was allowed to read.

The information gleaned from the pages of these old magazines introduced me to another world, a world inhabited by kings and queens and the rich and famous who seemed to lead such enchanted lives. This is how I got to read the story about the conquest of Mount Everest, the coronation of Queen Elizabeth II, though a brief announcement regarding the two events of 1953 were given to us during morning chapel. At this period however, I could read only bits and pieces of the magazine through the courtesy of some of my classmates. But when we started spending Saturday mornings in the school library, I had free access to the old copies and spent many hours engrossed in the language as well as the contents of this fine magazine. This is how *Time* magazine became my favourite foreign magazine later; I bought them when I could, or else borrowed it from friends when funds were low. I admired the magazine for its coverage of a wide range of subjects and their usage of the English language which I believe was of immense help for enhancing my knowledge of and engendering an abiding love for this language.

The reading rage that grew in me is also due to the Saturday study hours when I could go to the school library and read whatever caught my fancy on a given morning. Because of this habit which has by now grown into an obsession, I can cope better with the necessary boredom and loneliness that is a part of our human existence. I sometimes have nightmares about being stranded in a lonely place without a book!

Glee Club

During our first year of high school, the principal announced that she was going to form a Glee Club where the members would be taught to sing in harmony from musical notations. I always liked to sing and was absolutely thrilled by the announcement. Without a moment's hesitation, I decided to volunteer for the club.

On a Saturday evening the principal called us to her bungalow for an 'audition'! We were made to sing the notes as she played them on the piano and I saw that against each name she was jotting down some remarks. At the end of the exercise, almost all of us were inducted into the choir and assigned the different parts that we were to sing. I got to be in the second soprano section. The division of the parts was somehow new to us. Earlier, the parts in choir singing were referred to as soprano, alto, bass and tenor. But in the American system, the different parts were designated as soprano, second soprano, first alto and second alto. Though I could not reproduce the high notes during the 'audition', I was taken in the second soprano group. It was only much later that I realized that the other point in my favour was that I could read piano notation and play out the tunes. For several of the songs the Glee Club presented at special church services, the principal wrote down the notes for second soprano and instructed me to learn the part by heart on the piano and teach it to the others in this group.

Besides the few minutes of limelight we savoured while we sang on the pulpit of the church, the other attraction was the uniform that the club members were required to wear: white blouses with collars, white mekhela-chador or sari and a cute little black bow-tie on performance Sundays! Oh, how we lived for those days when we could perform on the pulpit not only in front of our fellow hostellers and teachers but also the entire congregation in the church! And it did not matter if a certain song sounded flat at a few points, we couldn't care less. We took pride in the fact that we stood on the pulpit and sang before a live audience. We did not mind giving up our leisure time for practice; instead, we felt that we were a class apart and felt privileged to be a member of the Glee Club!

But our glory days were soon to be over. I was in class IX and we were going to present a song in the Good Friday service of the local church. I do not know till today, why the principal chose that particular song, 'O Sacred Head Once Wounded', because it was a very difficult song. All other particulars of the song are long gone from my mind; only the title remains because performing that song proved to be such a disaster. It was composed on such a key that harmonizing the parts was very tricky. When I tried out the notes from the sheet handed to me by the principal, I knew that it was going to be tough to sing those notes in harmony with the rest. Too many flats, I thought but could not do anything else about it. So I spent long hours on the piano and tried to learn the second soprano part. When I tried to teach it to my group, I knew immediately that we were heading for a fiasco. But we had to sing it and so spent precious time taken out of study hours in attempting to master the notes.

The first time we tried singing all the parts together, we sounded terrible but the first sopranos somehow carried us through the entire three verses. We could see that the principal was worried but she gave us two more days to fine-tune all the parts. Good Friday was soon with us and two days before the service we were called to the bungalow and made to rehearse the song several times. Some semblance of harmony was emerging out of our efforts and our spirits perked up. The principal gave us a rare smile and said that Thursday evening would be the final practice.

Thursday practice went off without a flat note anywhere and we felt on top of the world after so much of agony and uncertainty. The principal was literally grinning. Then came the great day, and we of the Glee Club marched at the head of the column of hostellers walking two by two to the local church all decked out in our white outfits, with a little black bow-tie tucked into our collars. Special numbers from our Glee Club were always a welcome diversion for the congregation; it provided relief from the regular monotony of the service. We could see the expectation on the faces of the audience as we marched into the church. The large congregation was waiting eagerly for us to mount the pulpit and regale them with the number.

As on other occasions, when the song was announced, we marched to the pulpit in the order of our singing parts, the principal stood before us with her song sheet and holding a tiny baton with which to direct the choir. On a queue from the tiny stick, we started our song and immediately, a sense of doom descended on my heart because it became clear that the main note to be carried by the first sopranos was off-key. We somehow got through the first verse; but because of the wrong key in the beginning, the second verse started on a different note to which the other parts could not adjust mid-stream and by the time the song ended, I could see that the principal's face had turned absolutely red. Earlier in the second verse I saw her giving frantic signals to the first sopranos on whom depended the harmony of the rest but there was no way anyone could do anything about it at that stage. It was not a practice session; it was the *performance*! If there had been some accompaniment with musical instruments, our discordant voices would somehow have been camouflaged by the music. But it was only our voices we had to rely upon and we found ourselves totally lost in our own cacophony as the song ended on terribly discordant notes. We returned to our benches shame-faced and bewildered wondering how we could have done so badly on this important day. After this fiasco, the Glee Club remained more or less defunct and I honestly do not remember whether it continued or our debacle on that fateful Friday sealed its doom.

When I reflect on this experience, I begin to wonder what prompted me to opt for this group when I knew that I was not in any way a good singer. And more importantly, I also wonder why I was included in the club. Sure I could hold a tune, but there is an essential difference in being technically correct on a note and being able to infuse harmony and soul into the notes. Also, it was not as if we were the pick of the lot; come to think of it, as far as I remember, we were the only lot who volunteered and except for one or two she chose the rest of the volunteers. But whatever be the reason, by inducting us into this club, she did introduce us to the world of vocal music, and gave us something to look forward to away from the tedium of school work and hostel chores. For those brief moments, we did feel special and I recall this with a deep sense of gratitude to our Principal who tried to give us some good memories of our school days. Except for the Good Friday debacle, I believe that our club did present some decent special numbers in church through our harmonized voices.

At this point, I recall another act of kindness of the Principal when I had just joined the hostel. She must have noticed that I wore the same frock to school five days a week.

She stopped me one day on my way from school and gave me a packet containing a length of cloth. She also instructed me to tell a particular senior girl to make a frock out of it for me. I ran to the hostel with the packet and locating the girl, gave the message to her. She immediately set to work and by the next day, the frock was ready! I still remember the pattern: there were pale green vertical lines against a beige background and I wore it proudly because it was a gift from the Principal.

Cooking Classes

Cooking simple dishes was treated as practicals in our Domestic Science class. We were divided into groups and on certain days taken to an empty kitchen meant for visiting teachers where the teacher in-charge gave demonstrations. I remember that our first lesson was making an egg curry with four eggs and two potatoes. Then came the lesson on making pakoras and bhajia. I still remember the yellow twists of the besan dough plopping into the hot oil through a press full of holes and turning crisp right before our eyes. The last lesson I remember was making plum jelly and the process of bottling it in sterilized jars. It was my favourite lesson because it involved such a lovely colour. After my marriage, I made countless jars of this wonderful jelly with the plums from my mother-in-law's orchard. And I enjoyed distributing these jars to all the relatives and friends. It was at first rumoured that those of us who were involved in these classes were considered to be lucky because we would get to taste the goodies that we made. But we were in for a big disappointment; all the finished products went to the Principal's table and the best we could do was to lick the pans and taste the jelly from the ladle!

Hawaiian Sandals

Shoes, as you will remember were a forbidden item in our school, church and hostel as well. But it did not mean that the girls did not have a pair tucked away at the bottom of their trunks to be taken out and worn the moment they crossed the school boundary on their way home during vacations. No such luxury for me however; no shoes meant literally NO shoes. I did not own even a battered pair because when I left home my brother took out my only serviceable shoes out of my trunk as he was told that shoes were not permitted in the school.

I may have been one of the poorest girls in the hostel and I was there because of my impoverished and orphaned status. But there was also a class of girls in the school who had rich parents who could have given their daughters anything they wanted or could have sent them to any posh school of their choice. But they were sent to this boarding school because of its strict discipline and more importantly, the quality of education that the girls received here. Among the day scholars also, there were daughters of the elite of the town and they were all non-Christians. In that sense I should have felt privileged to be in such a school. But at that age I saw only my poverty and the others' material advantages. These were the girls who appeared to be the favourites with the Super and the Matron. They were visited often by their parents and they were allowed to keep the presents they received. This fact always put me on the defensive and I envied their seeming exclusivity, and at the same time resented the special treatment they received from the Super and the Matron and I grew increasingly hostile towards them.

It was the early fifties, the period when nylon and terrylene had become the rage. So were Hawaiian sandals. It was whispered in the hostel that a girl called Bobby had received such a pair and used to wear them during evening study hour. I was burning with curiosity to see this wonder and plotted to have a glimpse of it without anybody seeing me. On a particular evening I walked to the study room before anybody else and went straight to her desk and pulled out the sandals from the bottom. Even now I distinctly remember the blue colour, how it felt in my hands and above all how the rubber smelt! While thus lost in awe and admiration of this wonder, I did not hear Bobby come in. Only when she shouted "Hey what are you doing?" did I become aware of her presence. By that time some other girls had straggled in and were looking at the sorry spectacle of my humiliation unfolding before their eyes.

My face still burns with the shame and chagrin I felt that evening on being discovered holding someone else's property in my hands and being 'caught red-handed', as it were. The worst part was that it was the owner who'd caught me at this most embarrassing moment of my life! Without saying anything I dropped the sandals and went to my desk on the other side of the room but not before I saw the smirk on her face as if she was saying, 'These are things you should never even look at!" I've never felt so small and poor as at that moment and I still think that my poverty was somehow demeaned by my action. The episode of the Hawaiian sandals was to haunt me for a very long time and for a long time I could not look at this girl without wincing inwardly.

The only pair of shoes I owned in the hostel so far was a hand-me-down from a senior girl who got fed up with them and casually handed them to me. I hid them at the bottom of my trunk and used to wear them to church when I went to the village. They were ill-fitting and looked old but I persisted in wearing them at every opportunity. On those occasions I also knew that girls my age including my own cousins were walking behind me and making fun of me walking about unsteadily in those old and clumsy shoes. But I did not care. After every experience like that I would sit quietly at home and long for a brand new pair which would fit me properly. And then on an impulse one day I wrote a letter to my maternal aunt Senlila who was undergoing training to become a staff nurse in the Medical College in Dibrugarh, Assam telling her of my 'need' and giving her my shoe-size which was Bata four and half. A long time passed and I forgot all about the letter.

But then one day the Super called me and gave me a parcel which I had to open before her. And lo and behold! There was a pair of red Bata shoes from my aunt which fitted me perfectly. It must have been the latest design, with slightly elevated crepe soles with back straps. For me they were the most wonderful gift in a life always hankering after things that I remembered possessing when my parents were alive. The Super glared at me and warned that if I was caught wearing them, I would be punished and the shoes confiscated. But I still remember the thrill and joy of owning such a beautiful pair of shoes even though I had to wait till I went to the village for the winter holidays to be able to wear them. Till today I remember that pair of red shoes with eternal gratitude to my aunt.

Talking of shoes, I often wonder if childhood deprivations grow into adult fetishes, but then I am sure that Imelda Marcos never had a miserable childhood like mine!

The Swing

Having to cope with the tough schedule of duties as a hosteller and the ever-increasing load of studies to be covered, there was hardly any leisure to feel sorry for oneself and indulge in self-pity for long or even feel envious of those girls who seemed to have more in life than me. And yet there were times when I could not help feeling depressed and lonely. Whenever these moods overtook me, I used to sit out on one of the swings in the hostel compound after dark and try to banish all thought from my mind. At times when I was too agitated and felt like screaming, I would stand on the wooden board of the swing and start moving back and forth. The more I swung, the more relaxed I felt and there were quite a few times when I increased the pace so much that I nearly went above the iron bar from which the swing was suspended. These moments were terrifying and exhilarating at the same time. But sometimes the high swinging motions on the swing would bring on bouts of nausea which had a sobering effect on me and I would go in to my House a calmer person.

Swinging high, almost over the bars, I used to think that I could touch the stars with just one more push of my feet on the board but some instinct pulled me back each time and I would be content with the promise to myself, 'May be next time.'

These solitary moments over the chasm were the nearest that I ever came face to face with the great unknown, though at that time I could not articulate the formal word for such a deep longing for oblivion. But by the time I reached the IXth class, the attempted trysts with the stars gradually became less frequent and eventually stopped.

But to this day whenever I see an empty swing, I recollect how this simple contraption once provided me with wordless solace and also sometimes tempted me with the suggestion of ultimate escape from my misery.

Girl with the Creepy Hand

In high school, there was a much older girl in our class who, we were told, had a frightening stump for a right hand. Those who had accidentally seen it vouched that actually there was no hand; there were only five tiny globules pretending to be fingers on the stump where her wrist should have been. In an otherwise normal body it looked as if the creator had left an important part of her anatomy unfinished. Because of this, she wore her sari the 'wrong' way; instead of the pallu going over her left shoulder, it was draped over her right one and in such a way as to hide her deformity. Rumours began circulating that if you were touched with that hand, you would break out in rashes or worse. Because of the superstition attached to her deformity, she became almost a pariah and no one wanted to pair with her on our outings. As a result, she remained aloof and distant from most of the girls.

I could not believe that such abnormalities happened to people. The only instance that I had seen of something not being right in the human body were the legs of a baby boy in the children's ward of the hospital where I was once a patient myself. His legs did not seem to have any bones; he could twist them any way he wanted to, while lying on his back in the cot, he would put the toes in his mouth and play with the feet as if they were toys. Obviously he could not crawl or sit up; he just lay there in his cot with a smile on his face. He would pull his legs up to his head without any problem and sometimes would tuck them under his back to make them disappear. But as far as I could see, his legs were well-formed with all the toes in place as he lay in the hospital cot. For that hapless little boy, his useless legs in a way had become his plaything.

But here was a grown-up girl who had an abnormal right hand and had to do everything with her left including writing. I was totally overwhelmed by her problem; I wanted to know why and how this had happened to her. I wanted to talk to her about this and began to look for opportunities to be near her. I soon found out that she had problems with English grammar and the more difficult sums. So whenever I saw her struggling with these during study hours, I would quietly pass scraps of paper across to her desk with the answers. At first she was suspicious and reluctant to accept my offer of help but knowing that she would be in trouble if she did not have the right answers, she accepted my help. Slowly and steadily we were becoming close to each other. Sometimes she would pass me half a lozenge and I would nod thanks. I even volunteered to pair with her to church and on other rare outings. We made an incongruous pair: she was much taller than me, much darker and looked definitely older. Being the youngest and smallest in the class, I looked stunted beside her. But the physical differences did not deter me and I continued to be her mate on walks not only to church but on other outings also.

One evening during study hour, she gave me a poke and signalled for me wait till everyone had left the room. I deliberately hung back and as soon as we were alone, she motioned for me to come closer to her and with a flick of her left hand, lifted her pallu and showed me her stump. It was disconcerting at first, but I looked on, fascinated by this mistake of nature. The hand indeed had five tiny globules of flesh where the wrist should have been. Seeing my shocked face, she did a strange thing; she asked me, "Do you want to touch it?" Frightened as I was by the sight of the stump I took a step backwards as if to avoid touching it. She chuckled and said, "It's alright, I am myself afraid of it sometimes." Then she did a strange thing, she stroked my face ever so gently with those tiny mock-fingers and began to cry. I put my arm around her and let her cry for sometime. Then taking hold of her good hand we walked out of the room in silence and parted ways to go to our respective Houses without uttering a word. But both of us knew that a bond was forged between us at that moment when she was so willing and even unabashed to show me her freak hand. By that gesture she ushered me into her secret world and acknowledged me as her friend.

The next year when she came back from the Christmas holidays she brought me some ladoos made with sesame seeds and gur. They were delicious. This special girl was with us only up to class VIII. I missed her because we had become good friends without having to say much to each other. Even as I write this, I can still recall the fleeting sight of her un-finished right hand and feel the gentle pat as it caressed my face that night and I begin to understand what it must have been like to be shunned and dreaded by others for no fault of hers. She must have understood that I too was suffering from a similar sense of alienation and reached out to a kindred soul for mutual comfort.

I looked for her at the start of the next class but someone said that she would not come back. Her absence hurt for a while but the pain soon dissipated in the flurry of activities that followed as I was once again immersed in studies and the various duties in the hostel. By and by my association with her became a thing of the past and eventually almost forgotten, until I began reminiscing about my years in the school. Recalling this particular association has made me realize that deprivation can be of many different types but the suffering is the same as we both understood each other's pain through our silent communication.

As I write about my special friendship with this girl, the creepy hand becomes irrelevant; what I remember and cherish is the warmth of her welcoming gesture with that aberration of nature. I only hope that she found other friends and fulfilment in life.

Nakham and the Missing Guavas

Life in the hostel was tough but we managed to make our existence slightly more tolerable by indulging in certain actions fraught with risk and at the same time which provided us with some diversionary fun.

There was this incident in the 1st House when I was there as a junior. One girl had somehow managed to smuggle some dry fish or 'nakham' as it was called in her language when she came back from the holidays. She spoke about eating it constantly and the other tribal girls understood what she was implying because this is a delicacy with us too; especially when you make chutney out of it with chillies and tomatoes. No meal at home would be complete without this side dish. She kept on saying that she was homesick and unless she cooked and ate the nakham, her homesickness would not disappear! So she began to plan for this 'prohibited' operation: hostellers were not allowed to cook anything of their own in the kitchen or anywhere else within the compound.

On a Saturday afternoon, she and a few of her friends somehow got hold of an empty tin and pilfering some salt and chilli from the larder began to cook the nakham in the kitchen. Soon the whole area began to smell of the fish; but she carried on happily until someone shouted, 'Matron'. All the other girls disappeared from the scene leaving her alone. Unperturbed, she took the tin, went to the fence and deposited it behind some bushes.

Hurrying into the kitchen, she started abusing an imaginary mongrel blaming it for the stink of what he had done and which she was pretending to clean by throwing buckets of water on the kitchen floor as well as the fireplace to douse the recently lit fire. By the time the Matron entered much of the stink was gone and the girl was mopping the floor with a dry cloth, mumbling curses at the non-existent dog. The Matron simply peeped at what was going on and went away grumbling that her mid-day nap was disturbed for nothing.

As soon as she was gone, the girl ran to the fence and brought back the tin with nakham and without waiting for her accomplices, ate up the half-cooked stinking concoction and threw the tin beyond the fence shouting, "Oye, my home-sickness is gone!"

By the time the other girls re-assembled after the Matron's departure, they discovered that she had finished the dish all by herself. What they said when they realized that they had missed the treat, does not bear repeating! But by now satiated girl was heard yelling at them, "Serves you right for deserting me."

Now when I think about this episode, it makes me realize the importance of the association of food items to different cultures of the world. We know that often what seems to be stinky, ugly and inedible to some is a delicacy to others. This particular dry fish called 'nakham' has a very strong smell which is offensive to some but for many others it is a much relished delicacy. No meal is complete without this side-dish. Thus the association of food to nationalities is a world-wide phenomenon. For example, when you say 'curry', the nationality that invariably comes to mind is 'Indian'; one could go on adding to the list of such associations. In that sense perhaps, for this girl 'nakham' was a strong reminder of home, and hence her intense urge to taste a bit of that 'home' in the impersonal hostel environment was so overwhelming that she did what she did. The episode which in our young minds was a hilarious bit of mischief, acquires quite a different significance when viewed from this perspective now.

And then there was this episode of the missing guavas from Miss's garden. The crop that year was bountiful and

the guavas were ripening a beautiful yellow right in front
of our eyes, the branches bending over with the weight
of their treasure. How our mouths watered each time we
crossed the tree on our way to and from school! They
seemed so tantalizingly within our grasp. Incidentally, that
was the period when I had a few followers who had attached
themselves to me somehow and we had become a gang of
sorts. Some were my classmates and some senior to me.
I knew that if I proposed something, they would help me
carry out the plan.

When I broached the subject of stealing some guavas,
they enthusiastically agreed. So, choosing a dark evening
three of us, expert tree-climbers, shimmied up the fruit-
laden tree, plucked the biggest ones of the lot and scrambled
down and ran towards the far end of the compound where
the bath-houses were located. We sat down on the grass in
the darkness and divided the guavas among the six of us. We
got to eat three big guavas each. And oh! how we relished the
sweet taste of the juicy fruit!

But there was a sequel to this adventure. When the theft
was discovered, the first suspects were of course our gang
members because we had earned some kind of notoriety by
then as potential troublemakers in the hostel. But the Super,
who surely knew that I was the leader did not confront me,
whether out of aversion or fear of some retaliatory remark
from me, I cannot say. She stopped another member of the
gang named Libeni on her way from school and asked, "Hey
Libeni, what happened to my guavas?" Though this girl was
small in stature and looked mild, there was fire in her too.
So she looked her straight in the eye and answered calmly,
"How should I know anything about your guavas? Ask your
chowkidar" and walked off. That was the last we heard about
Miss's missing guavas!

The Mango Trick

When I was in the IXth class I was made a Mahi (or monitor in current parlance). This was unusual because normally only class X students were selected for this job. I was put in the 3rd House which was situated closer to the well and bathhouses. Also there were more trees like jackfruit and mango behind the House. Every Mahi was accountable for the general conduct of the girls and the cleanliness of the House and kitchen and also its surroundings. She would also have to maintain strict discipline among the inmates regarding lights-out, evening service on certain days and compliance with any instructions received from the Matron from time to time. Though there were a few class X girls in our House, I got on well with them and even if they had any resentment against me on account of having to listen to a junior, they never showed it. But my problem was with the Super ever since the time I came to the hostel. It began with the incident when I was punished in front of visitors for sending a girl to her father without prior permission from her.

Whenever the Super came on inspection visits to our House, she would always find ways to scold me for the flimsiest of reasons which made me look irresponsible and incapable of handling my job. I felt miserable and thought of getting even with her somehow or the other.

Then came the mango season and one day the Super came to class with a swollen face and eyes with heavy lids almost closing over them. Later we came to know that she was allergic to mangoes and had inadvertently walked past a tree laden with young fruit. She looked horrible and we sympathized with her. And then suddenly this fact gave me a wicked idea. I thought how marvellous it would be if some green mangoes were placed on her way to our house to make her turn away when she came for Saturday inspection!

I decided to try the trick and managed to collect some mangoes which had fallen from the tree and kept them aside and when it was time for her regular visit, placed a few of them in strategic positions on her way. When she saw the first mango, she stopped in her track and ordered it removed. But the sight of the second one made her turn around and stomp away telling the Matron to finish the inspection. For the entire summer she delegated the inspection work to the Matron and the 3rd House heaved a collective sigh of relief. But this was only one example of my personal conflict with the Super which was to continue all through my stay in the hostel.

Vacations

We used to get a month's holiday every summer and while the other girls could not wait for the holidays to begin, it was misery time for me because I had nowhere to go. The only place I could go was our village where my elder brother was working as a school teacher and my younger siblings, three of them, were with him in our uncle's house. It was impossible to travel to our village during the summer because all the rivers and streams would be in spate and there were no bridges over them. It was the fifties and there were no motorable roads, people had to walk all the way to and from their villages. Only during winters, the rivers could be crossed at their shallow stretches and villagers would walk to the markets in the plains to stock up on salt and kerosene during these months. It was also the time when they could make a little money by selling their home grown produce like oranges, ginger and betel leaves in the small markets at the foot-hills. So going to the village during summer was out of the question.

It so happened that the daughters of an old friend of my father were also in our school and we had become quite friendly. They told their father about my plight and on hearing this he approached the Superintendent and offered to take me to their home for the holidays. When I was told about this, I could not believe my sheer good fortune in being rescued from a hot and lonely summer and I suppose even the Super was relieved to be rid of me as I would have been the only hosteller for a whole month.

The excitement and the sense of freedom however soon disappeared when we reached the last railway station where we had to disembark to walk the rest of the way to our destination, the home of my benefactor. There was only a jungle path which gradually became steeper and steeper as we climbed the hills. On our way we passed a place called Borjan where coal mining was going on. We could see the trolleys on the ropeways transporting the coal to the dumping ground near the railway depot. How I wished we could travel on those contraptions on their way up for the next load!

By the time we managed to reach the outskirts of a village called Kongen, our legs felt like lead and we were gasping for breath. But a greater shock than physical exhaustion awaited me as we entered the village. For the first time in my life, I saw practically naked women walking about in broad daylight. They wore only the skimpiest of skirts around their waist while their upper bodies were bare, except for the many strings of coloured beads that hung around their necks, falling in a cascade over their breasts. Not only that, they all had black teeth! It was only much later that I was told that black teeth were considered beautiful among this tribe and therefore these women tinted their teeth with natural dye extracted from certain leaves, bark and roots from the jungle. Even the men sported black teeth. We rested in the house of a friend of the family for sometime where the hosts gave us some sweet tea which revived us somehow. But we had to march on because we had reached only the half-way point of our trek. The sun had almost set and we reached the village called Wakching as darkness was enveloping the hillsides where this good man and his family lived. He had started out as a teacher in the Christian High School at Jorhat and went on to become an ordained missionary among the Konyak Nagas and was stationed in this village called Wakching, now slowly developing into a township. For the first time since my parents died I was in a real home with a family who took me in and gave me love and shelter. This was the home of the Late Rev. Longri Ao and his lovely wife Aunty Subokumla. They had six children: the eldest one whom we called Kaka, is named Imkongtemsu, (a fine guitarist and civil servant) then a daughter who was called Watisungla but was Didi for us, then a son called Imchalemba (who later joined politics both at State and central levels, has been Lok Sabha member, state legislator and Minister too), then two more daughters Sungtirenla and Lanusanenla (also known as Sunny Chuba, the All India Radio personality) and a youngest son Yubanganglemba, (a civil engineer of repute).

I spent two summer vacations with this family and though I dreaded the tortuous walk up hill paths to our destination, the happy atmosphere and good food made up for the strenuous journey. I spent happy days with the family. We went to local football matches and of course attended regular church services on Sundays. The missionary was a very jolly person and he used to entertain us with stories and jokes after dinner and sometimes we played ludo or snakes and ladders. It was amusing to hear his daughters sometimes screaming at him saying he was cheating! Imagine a missionary cheating at ludo! I remember an anecdote narrated by the missionary about some early converts during one after-dinner chat. He said that a group of them came to him on a Saturday asking him to excuse them from Sunday's service because they were all taking 'leave' to go to their fields to sow seeds. When asked why they could not do it on Monday, they replied that the most suitable day for sowing fell on that Sunday according to their traditional lunar calendar! They added that if they missed it, their crops would fail. They were converts no doubt, but it seems that their concept of Sunday as a special day reserved for the new god had not settled deep enough in their minds yet.

Once we went to the field of a member of the church where we were offered freshly plucked corn roasted over an open wood fire. Along with it we ate the sweetest and most succulent cucumbers, also freshly plucked from the field. We had the feast sitting on the verandah of the field hut. But when I entered the kitchen, a shocking sight greeted me. Over the fireplace Nagas usually hang a contraption made of bamboo where meat or fish is dried for preservation. But what I saw on this particular bamboo tray was neither of these, there were big rats split open vertically, the openings held in place by wedging pieces of twig and bamboo across, and spread on the tray to dry! The creatures were much bigger than the domestic variety that I was familiar with but they were rats all the same and the sight nearly made me throw up. The missionary's family however did not seem affected by the sight. Later I was told that rats caught in the jungle were a delicacy for the Konyaks.

It was during my first stay with this family that I sent a letter to Mrs Hasselblad asking her to send me a pair of shoes. I did not receive any reply and soon forgot about it. But back in school after the vacation, I was summoned one day by the Super and asked why I had written such a letter to Mrs. Hasselblad. I was flabbergasted; I never thought that this kind lady would put me in such a situation at school. But luckily for me the Super simply scolded me for writing the letter and sent me back to the hostel without 'punishing' me for posting an uncensored letter!

I also remember that while cleaning the glass frame of a hurricane lamp, it slipped from my soapy hands and broke into pieces. I was terrified of what Aunty would say, and sure enough, she became almost incoherent with anger and frustration. I did not know what to do and burst into tears. At that point of time I thought that the fuss for a glass frame was a little exaggerated. It is only in retrospect that I understand why Aunty was so upset. The replacement could not be bought in the village; to get even the simplest things like salt, matchboxes, soap and kerosene, one had to trudge all the way to the border town of Naginimara, an entire day's march and back. Life was indeed extremely tough those days and the broken glass shade meant there would be one less lantern for the family for many days until the replacement was procured. In retrospect I realize how truly generous and magnanimous this family was to have welcomed me into their midst for two consecutive summers, fed me and looked after me like their own. I also remember, Aunty even stitched some much-needed inner garments for me from her own stock of cloth. I shall always remember the happiness of being with the family because their spontaneous acceptance of me and their warmth made me forget that I had no family of my own.

Another incident that happened during one of these vacations has remained in my mind for all these years. There was a big CYE (Christian Youth Endeavour) convention being held at Wakching, the place where we were. Many delegates from neighbouring villages had come to participate. It was, most probably, held over several days. As in all such gatherings, the concluding night's service was going to be very special. In order to make the occasion even more special, the organizers decided to request a special song from the Reverend's family. When we were told, we did not know what to do because none of us knew any song that could be sung as a group. Aunty had a lovely voice and often used to sing in the church, but this time she refused by saying that it was a convention for the youth and the children had to sing. We were all very subdued and worried as the day for the special service drew closer. The family was plunged into gloom as no one seemed to know how to tackle this huge challenge thrown at the missionary by his congregation. I do not remember who had this brainstorm, but someone timidly suggested that we could sing a very popular Hindi song from a film because no one would know the song for what it was! At first the Reverend was aghast: sing a Hindi movie song at a Christian convention as a special number from a missionary's family? Never, he fumed. By the next morning however, he seemed to have re-considered his initial reaction, mainly because time was running out. He called the children and asked us to sing the song before he made up his mind. We sang it with gusto because we knew most of the song by heart and in places where we forgot the words, we improvised. He must have been impressed because he called his eldest son and ordered him to accompany us with his guitar! Having obtained his go-ahead we practiced the song several times and sang that song in the evening service to enthral the audience. We were greeted with loud clapping after the song and I am sure that no one in that audience had the slightest clue about the origin or nature of the song!! All the same it turned out to be a huge success. By the way the song was, *Oh, oh, bachapan ke din bhula na dena, aj hasay kal rola na dena* from the movie 'Deedar' (1951)

Apart from the natural hindrance caused by flooded rivers which made it impossible to travel to my village during summer, there was another development which added to the problem. By the mid fifties the Naga Freedom movement had started in earnest and violent encounters between the insurgents and security forces made the hills almost

inaccessible and extremely dangerous. It was fortuitous that
by that time, my father's cousin named Mayangmeiba had
admitted his daughters Alice and Asangla in our boarding
school. So it fell on him, being a close relative, to take me
along with his daughters to the tea garden called Dikhari
where he was employed. It was thus that I spent the first
three summer holidays of my high school years with them
in the tea garden. What I remember from the vacations
spent there are beautifully manicured rows of tea plants,
the sahib's bungalow with sprawling grounds, the little
huts where the labourers lived and also the little circle of
Christian families who worked there. There was even a small
church made of bamboo and thatch where we assembled
for Sunday services. My aunt was a nurse in the infirmary
and sometimes I would walk over to the small dispensary to
watch her administer to the patients. It was very peaceful
there but somewhat isolated from the main population of
the small town nearby.

One of the two incidents that I remember vividly from
this period was a visit to the factory where tea leaves were
made. This was done at certain times of the year and
required twenty-four hour supervision, otherwise, we were
told that whole bunches of leaves could go waste resulting in
enormous losses to the company. During these periods, my
uncle would be away from home for several days as he had
to do careful monitoring of the several stages through which
the freshly plucked tea leaves would be processed to produce
the required quality. I still find it an odd designation, but my
uncle was called Second Tea House Babu. One summer, he
arranged for us, the three girls, to go and see how things
were done. So on the appointed day we went to the factory
and watched the leaves being dried on huge shifting trays
and conveyor belts, then loaded on the grinders and sent
on to some other conveyor belts to separate the different

kinds of tea. It was an awe-inspiring experience to see the green tea leaves changing colour as they were subjected to different degrees of heat and how the final product looked so different.

We were told that it was during this time that vigilance was most stringent in the garden because the smuggling of tea leaves in the labourers' pockets out of the factory was quite common. When the bell rang at the end of the day, they had to file past a guard at the gate with their shirt and pants pockets turned inside out! In spite of such measures, uncle told us, that some clever guys still managed to smuggle some tea leaves under their armpits or in the folds of their trousers.

The other incident that I remember from my garden holidays was the sight of small boys holding empty condensed milk tins going in and out of the rows of tea plants. At first I thought that they were playing some sort of game, but later came to know that they were collecting the green worms that feed on tea leaves. When the tins were full of these worms, they would take them to the sahib who would pay them four annas for every tin of worms! An ingenuous way of getting rid of the pests and a marvelous way of earning four annas with a little labour!

There was yet another incident which I often recall and have a good laugh even if I am alone. I have shared this with my children and friends too, much to their amusement. It happened on a Sunday when uncle decided to take us to a town called Dibrugarh, which is not too far from the tea garden. It was also an opportunity to meet my youngest maternal aunt Senlila who was undergoing training in the Dibrugarh Medical College to become a staff nurse. I remember we travelled in a jeep. After meeting with my aunt, the three of us clamoured to see the Sunday matinee show in town. Uncle and aunty relented but by the time we

entered the hall, the show had begun; the trailer section was
being shown. Our seats were on the balcony row and much
to the irritation of the others we noisily proceeded to our
places and hurriedly sat down. But after a while when our
eyes got adjusted to the dimness of the hall, I discovered that
the three of us were perched much higher than the others,
uncle and aunty included. I nudged Alice and whispered,
'Why are we so high?' She fumbled at the seat and laughed
out loudly; every body around us hissed and told us to be
quiet. I too fumbled at my seat and realized that we were
perched on seats that were folded upright and we had sat
on them without unfolding them! We tried to suppress
our giggles but the more we tried the more hysterical we
became. In the meantime uncle was becoming 'furiouser'
and 'furiouser' and aunty was sitting beside him in acute
embarrassment at our behaviour. When the Interval came,
uncle marched us out of the hall and said that we were
going back immediately but aunty protested saying that
she was hungry. So we all shuffled to a nearby restaurant
and ordered lunch. It was during the meal that I wanted to
break the ice and told uncle, timidly at first, why we were
laughing. When he heard what I said, his facial expression
changed and he had to put down his spoon because he too
started to laugh. We were all relieved and our meal ended in
a jovial mood. All in all, it was a memorable Sunday outing,
but till today, I do not remember anything about the movie,
not even the title!

I spent three summer vacations at this tea garden with
my cousins. But when uncle came to fetch his daughters
for the next vacation, he said that for some reason I could
not go with them. I was totally devastated; I had nowhere
else to go! Not only that, I thought of it as some kind of
rejection for which I felt deeply ashamed. However, I hung
around the group of parents and students who were sorting

out luggage and saying goodbye to each other. Just then a lady who knew my parents spotted me and asked if I was going anywhere for the vacation. When she learnt that I had nowhere to go, she immediately went to the Super and offered to take me to her home along with her daughter who was in a junior class. And so, once again an unseen power opened a way for me to spend the summer with another family. The lady's name was Imtiongdangla and she was a distant relative of father's.

This family lived in a place called Dergaon in Assam where uncle, whose name was Imtinungkum, was a Deputy Superintendent of Police. It was a unique experience for me to live so close to the activities of the policemen and to see the strict observance of discipline within the different levels of the force. Aunty was an expert seamstress and she made good money from her labours. She often took us to see movies and bought trinkets for the two of us from her private earnings whenever we accompanied her to the market. I still remember the blouse she made for me that summer. The material was nylon and coloured deep blue with a tiny white floral pattern. It was the first coloured blouse that I wore and was a prized possession for many years.

As I look back on these experiences, I realize how these good-hearted and generous people eased my sense of deprivation and made me welcome in their homes and taught me the valuable lesson of 'giving' from the heart. But for their kindness and generosity of heart, I would have spent many more lonely vacations in the hostel and become more morose and depressed.

Village Interludes

The Christmas vacations during the winter were of a shorter duration and I did go to our village several times. My elder brother would come to fetch me from the hostel and we would travel either by bus or train to the last station after which we had to *walk* to the village. But it was an entire day's walk, which meant that we had to start very early the next morning. Our trip from the hostel to this point took most of the day and therefore we had to spend the night somewhere. I remember the details of only one such overnight stay at a place called Sonowal which is a tea-garden town in Assam.

For the villagers, winter was the time to visit the plains to purchase essential commodities like salt and kerosene. And because they needed shelter for at least two nights when they came down on such trips, they made arrangements with local residents for simple accommodation. The custom among the village folk was that they would carry provisions for the number of days they intended to stay out and so their need was simple: a place to sleep at night and some space to cook their meals. They always carried their own utensils and before reaching their destination on the way from the village, they would stop in the forest on the edge of town and collect enough firewood for cooking. When they went on such trips, they also formed groups of threes and fours so that the burden of carrying the firewood and utensils could be shared. If there were four persons in a group, each would carry one utensil, thereby lessening the burden. When cooking time came, each would measure out his/her share of the rice to be cooked. In short it was a co-operative effort aimed at more efficiency.

On his trip from the village to pick me up me from school, my brother had joined such a group. He had also carried provisions for the two of us. Everything worked according to plan on the onward journey. But when we reached the halting station on our way back from my school, there was a problem: where would I sleep? I could not join the women's group because every inch of space was taken up and obviously I could not join my brother's group. Incidentally, the 'space' here was the floor of a barn or empty cowshed where everyone used the single blankets they carried. Winters in the plains can be harsh and a thin blanket was not adequate to keep the cold out. But the villagers were no strangers to hardship and they gratefully accepted the bare hospitality offered by poor farmers like themselves. No money exchanged hands in these transactions; but when the hill people collected firewood to cook their meals, they often carried an extra bundle for their host. Or when they harvested the next ginger or orange crops they would set aside some for their 'Assamiya mitro' when they went on their next shopping trip. Friendships thus cultivated through mutual need have lasted for many years even after roads were constructed and overnight halts at small towns on the foothills became a thing of the past.

But to come back to the predicament I faced regarding a bed that night: after much discussion with the host, a strange bed was found for me. The owner of the house happened to be a Marwari shopkeeper who had known my parents and he agreed to give me a place to sleep. After the community meal my brother took me to the shop and said that I would be sleeping there. When I asked where, the shopkeeper pointed out to the loft under the roof which could be reached by climbing up a ladder. When I hesitated, my brother explained to me that it was the only space available and besides, he said it would be only for a few hours because we had to get up at 3 in the morning to cook not only our morning meal but lunch also and must be on our way by 4 am.

I understood that I had nowhere else to go, and so reluctantly I clambered on to the rickety ladder and made my tentative way upwards to my perch under the roof. There was no bed, only some straw was spread over the bamboo matting with a tattered blanket of the roughest wool on the straw. It was dark up there and I did not relish the idea of sleeping in such a 'bed'. But after the day's exertions, I did not have the luxury of fretting too much and fell asleep immediately and awoke only when my brother came to fetch me for our long walk to the village. It was still pitch dark but there was a lot of activity around several make-shift fireplaces where meals were being cooked. After the cooking was over, the fires were doused with water and the groups sat down to eat the first meal of the day. Then some food was packed into individual leaf packets for the mid-day meal. Then the groups got together and began to march towards the hills. Later on I learnt that such groups were formed on the basis of village neighbourhoods for convenience's sake and would disband once the journey was completed.

Except for my brother and me, all the others were carrying heavy loads of salt, kerosene tins, soap etc. in their conical shaped bamboo baskets slung around their foreheads with a bamboo strap. My brother carried my battered tin trunk and I was the only one without a load to carry. For the villagers, each step must have been agonizing but these expert climbers soon overtook us and went marching ahead as if they had no burden to carry. Another amazing thing I remember from this particular journey was they way they 'called' out words like 'hohe', 'hai' and 'hui' which created a rhythm of sorts for their march. For them it was a routine they followed whenever they marched, either from the shopping expeditions or carrying paddy home from far-flung fields or fetching fire-wood etc. I suppose it was a novel way of relieving the monotony of a silent march and this way the 'callers' could account for each member of the group during the day-long march in the deep jungle.

There must have been such other incidents of overnight halts whenever I came to spend Christmas vacation with my siblings in the village but details of this particular journey have stayed in my mind perhaps on account of my 'lofty' accommodation atop a Marwari shopkeeper's ceiling!

The short visits to the village during the winter vacations opened a completely new area of experience for me. I did not fully grasp it at that time but it now seems that I was moving between two diametrically opposite ways of life; life in the village was so different from the one I lived in the hostel. The village houses were built close together, the eaves of one house touching those of the next one. The traditional structure of the houses was the same: the first room on entry was the one where firewood was stacked against a wall; the perch for chickens on another and in the open space, there would be the big wooden mortar with a hole where paddy was husked with a heavy wooden pestle. Every village child learnt how to husk paddy as soon as s/he became old enough to hold a pestle. Incidentally, there would be pestles of several sizes, beginning with smaller and lighter ones for children and the heavier ones for adults. The mortars too were of different sizes, sometimes a big one would have up to five or six holes. Traditionally only the rich would have such big ones. In ordinary households the mortars would have only one or two holes. In this portion of the house, there was an opening constructed out of loose bamboo stakes which would be taken out to allow the family pigs to enter and feed in the mornings and evenings. During the day they would roam freely in the village and even outside its perimeter.

The next room could be entered by stepping over a barrier of about two feet which was placed there in order to prevent the chickens and pigs from entering the main house. This was the biggest room; on entering, the first corner on the left was reserved for the bamboo cylinders containing water, then there would be a shelf where earthen pots and bamboo leaf plates would be stacked. On this side there would be big earthen pots containing husked rice ready for cooking. The hearth was constructed almost in the middle of the room on a squarish portion plastered with earth on the bamboo floor. Touching the wall on the right beside the fireplace there would be two narrow wooden beds for the couple, placed head to head. The only private room of the house was a small cubicle at the end of this room which was for storing things like clothes, oil, soap, etc. and also for girls to change their clothes. The back door opened to a platform constructed with un-split bamboos which served as a working area: for sunning clothes, drying paddy and in a corner there was a small space walled off for bathing and washing.

Such houses are no longer to be found in the villages as they often caught fire and even otherwise had to be repaired frequently; they have been replaced by concrete structures with tin roofs. But during my short vacations in the village I stayed in such a house with my uncle, aunt, cousins and my brother who occupied the cubicle. All the children slept on bamboo mats around the fireplace.

Life in the village was hard, to say the least. We had to wake up at dawn to go and fetch water from the village wells, had to husk paddy when the adults went to the fields. Once a week, on Saturdays, we would carry all the dirty clothes in the house to the designated spot below the village well and wash them in the bitingly cold water. Incidentally, washing of clothes was not allowed near the wells where water was drawn for drinking and cooking. The wells being carved out of permanent natural sources, the excess would run down to lower ridges to form another well. Such lower wells were identified as washing areas.

But winter being the season of Christmas as well as weddings, I got to enjoy some fun during these vacations. Christmas was the biggest event in village life. Every household earmarked a pig to be slaughtered during this season and from around the 22nd of December, the early morning silence would be shattered by the squealing of pigs which were being speared to provide the goodies for the festive season. Perhaps because of this experience, for a very long time I associated the squealing of dying pigs with Christmas!

Christmas in the village was associated with another experience: carol singing in the village street, till midnight on 24th December. During one particular Christmas, I was taken in by an older cousin who had come to the village after several years. She had many friends who insisted that there should be carol singing that Christmas since she was a good singer. Though I was much younger than the group, my cousin insisted on having me along and I followed them meekly. By midnight every one was tired and almost frozen in the biting cold. So it was decided that we would go to a house and sit by the fire to revive us. One member of the group said his house was the nearest and we all trooped in to his kitchen and he made a big fire sitting around which we warmed ourselves. The blackened tea kettle, a permanent fixture in every hearth, soon began to bubble and we drank the hot black brew with lumps of molasses made by his mother from their own sugarcane. I still remember how the strong brew warmed us inside and the sweetness of the molasses revived our flagging energy. This combination is a typically 'village' repast when farmers take a break from their work in the fields or forests. But I know of many 'town' people who still enjoy this occasional relapse into their pre-modern repast! I must confess that I too enjoy this 'dehati' combination once in a while.

The other memorable experience of my village holidays was weddings. I got to attend quite a few during my vacations in the village because winter is the time for weddings in the hills. This is the time when the harvest is done, this is the time when shopping trips to the plains can be undertaken and this is the time when new houses can be built with seasoned bamboo and wood. The last is very important because when an Ao man marries, he cannot take his bride to his parents' home; he has to build a new house where he will set up a brand-new household from his wedding night onwards.

The kinds of weddings that I remember have now gone out of fashion and have become the stuff of story books even in the villages. Except for the actual church ceremony everything about weddings has now become totally different. To begin with: the invitation itself; it used to go out in the form of a leaf packet containing a betel nut wrapped in a betel leaf distributed by the maternal nephews. If the host wanted the entire family to come, there would be a whole nut; if not, only a half, indicating just the husband and the wife would be welcome. On the wedding day there would be hectic activities in both the houses. In both the groom's and the bride's houses a feast would be prepared for close relatives and immediate neighbours. The preparations would begin early on the day itself. Groups of women would assemble in each house and start husking paddy which had already been dried and kept ready for the purpose. It was fascinating to see these women chanting rhythmic calls as they pounded on the huge mortars with heavy pestles. I was amazed to see two women pounding into the same hole with alternate precision. Since so many people were husking, they would soon have the rice winnowed and sieved and ready for the pots. The cooking would be done in huge pots, several of them at the same time.

In the meantime, the men would kill and dress the pigs and start cooking the pieces of succulent meat in kerosene tins thoroughly cleaned and converted into cooking utensils for the day. The method of cooking meat for a big crowd was different: the longish meat pieces would be strung, in long bamboo strings with a knot on one end, meaty fat portions would be strung on separate strings and cooked in tins. All the spicy ingredients also would be put in. When the meat was done, it was put on to big winnowing baskets and sliced into medium pieces. The guests would squat in rows facing each other and the women would start serving the rice on leaves, then the men would follow by putting an exact number of meat and fat pieces on each leaf-plate. The water in which the meat was cooked would become the gravy which would be poured last onto every plate. Except for meat, one could have second helpings of rice and gravy. Whenever there were children among the guests, older people would gift them a piece of meat and by the time the meal was over, the children's plates would have several extra pieces to eat! Then the elders would fetch fresh leaves and wrap the 'gifts' into a bundle for the children to carry home. In this custom there was no concept of 'jutha' or 'unclean' associated with the gift. Instead it was considered to be a sign of love for the youngsters. After such feasts, it was normal to see children traipsing home happily swinging their bundles of 'love'. Believe me; I too swung a few of those in my time!

The actual wedding ceremony however took place in the evening only so that villagers need not lose a whole day's labour in the field. The ones I remember did not have too many people in the service; definitely less people than at the feast! After the short ceremony, the couple would walk out of the church accompanied by their friends and relatives to the new house which had been built by the groom ahead of the wedding date. Those were days without electricity and people held burning torches fashioned out of tightly bound bunches of reeds with a piece of kerosene-soaked cloth at one end to keep the fire going. It made quite an impression on me following those burning torches winding up and down the narrow and stony village paths leading to the new house.

But the main attraction for us children was the treat awaiting every one once the couple reached their new house. Earlier in the day women would cook pots of sticky rice onto which the fat of pork was burned and dripped and the same was made into big balls of steamy rice redolent with pork fat. The rice balls would then be wrapped in leaf packets and each guest would be given one gift-wrapped ball of sticky rice! For the children there was a bonus: when every one had received the treat the rest of the balls would be up for grabs when the basket was emptied on to the ground from a perch. Oh, how we scrambled for the precious leaf packets! I do not exactly remember what these rice balls tasted like. But what I do remember is the slow torch-lit walk to the new house and the sense of expectation of the fun ending with the mad melee for the left-over rice balls.

Lonely Christmas

During the six years that I spent in this boarding school, there was at least one Christmas when I could not go anywhere during the holidays. The fifties were turbulent times in our hills and one particular year my brother could not travel to the plains to take me home for Christmas. So I had to spend the holidays with a few other girls who also, for various reasons could not go home.

Life was dull in the winter days. We could sleep as late as we liked but had to fend for ourselves as usual, so not much of a change there. One incident from this particular winter has stayed in my mind, not because it was spectacular or happy but because it was so depressing. We were taken to visit the inmates of a government kala-azar hospital and made to sing Christmas songs in order to cheer them up. The patients were emaciated, their eyes were listless and many of them did not even bother to look at us when we were singing. Anyway, who wants to listen to some strange girls singing alien songs when one is at death's door?

It was not only the indifference of the patients and their appalling condition that upset me: I was trying to recollect what I had read in our Hygiene class about the disease and wondering whether we would be infected by breathing the same air, however short the duration was.

Of all the dumb and un-inspired outings that we were forced to go on, this remains the most depressing and senseless one in my mind. What good did it do the patients? Did they even understand the songs we sang? How did we feel after this visit? More morose and depressed. Even the Christmas feast could not dispel the gloom from our minds after seeing those emaciated patients with faces blackened by the disease. The sense of inevitable doom stayed in my mind for a long time and at times when I felt really low I began to think that I was just like the terminally ill patients.

For the Super of course it was different, I thought cynically, she had done her 'good deed' for the year. I suppose religion and religious zeal has many strange manifestations.

However, the aftertaste of gloom created by the hospital visit was somehow alleviated by an outing to witness and even participate in an outdoor enactment of the Nativity Scene in a field near the Pastor's house and afterwards, we were served some sweet tea and biscuits by the Pastor's family. For us who were always within defined boundaries, the evening's momentary freedom in the wintry outdoors did lift our spirits. But I still thought of the carol singing in our village the earlier Christmas walking up and down the length of the village paths and missed the session of drinking black tea with molasses in my cousin's house till the cocks crowed to remind us that Christmas day had arrived.

Since there was nothing that I could do about the present situation, I tried to enjoy the freedom of not having any homework and spent the days reading all kinds of books that I could lay my hands on. But on certain days I would simply loll on the bed and dream absurd dreams of a handsome man coming to take me away from the dreary existence in this hostel.

Reverend Sahu

During my high school days, probably when we were in class VIII, a famous Christian evangelist named Reverend Sahu visited the local church and began a Revival campaign. His mission was to revitalize the churches in the area. There were daily evening services in our church where he preached about Jesus and what one should do to attain eternal life through Him. He was a powerful and emotional speaker and he interspersed his sermons with details about his own life: how he got converted to Christianity and what that meant to him. One could see that he was reaching out to his listeners' hearts and minds through his sermons. Not only that, he also had a beautiful singing voice and sang for the audience at intervals encouraging them to sing along with him. He said that many of the songs, which were in Hindi, were composed by him. The hostellers were also taken to many of the evening services during that period. He was a charismatic speaker and at the end of each service following a highly charged speech, he would call members of the congregation to approach the pulpit to confess their sins and accept Christ as their Lord and Saviour. Many responded, weeping aloud their confessions and lying prostrate before this man of God who brought lost souls to the fold every day. Some even declared loudly that they would devote the rest of their lives in service to God and the church.

It was all so dramatic and contagious that this mass religious hysteria caught many of us in its grip and a few of us began debating whether we too should make such public declarations. Our impressionable minds were totally turned towards such a step and we were tottering on the brink of joining the band of marchers to the pulpit one evening with our confessions and pledges; we only needed the final push from someone bold enough to say, 'Let's do it'. None dared take this responsibility and we still debated. During a discussion after dinner one evening, a senior girl casually remarked that if one did that, one had to remain unmarried and would have nothing to do with boys any more.

This bit of information came as a shock to me and somehow cooled my escalating religious ardour. Just before the Reverend's arrival on the scene, I had begun to notice a local boy during Sunday services and was gradually becoming infatuated with the idea of being in love with him. It was both exciting and terrifying at the same time. I would look for him every time I went to church and after spotting his seat, it would take all my determination not to glance at him too frequently. If anyone got a whiff of my fanciful thinking, it would be the end of my life, I thought. I couldn't bear the thought of exposure and humiliation before my peers, teachers and family. I would be branded as a 'loose' girl like I heard some girls in higher classes being described for daring to look at boys. I had nothing to indicate that he noticed me or even knew that I existed. But to renounce this new sensation all for the vague promise of rewards in another life did not seem so appealing anymore. However strong the mesmerizing quality of Rev. Sahu's preaching was, it had to contend with a growing girl's physical awakening and the natural attraction towards the opposite sex. Confused by such internal turmoil, I found that the power of his charismatic proclamations was slowly beginning to lose the initial appeal and hold on my imagination.

During school hours also, I could not help thinking about

the 'sacrifice' I had to make if I were to heed to the call of the preacher at the end of his sermon. The tempting invitation to the pulpit strongly appealed to my newly heightened religious fervour. But when I thought about the 'afterwards', I saw only a void. We were not sure what would happen even if we did make the public declaration. Would anyone take us seriously? If yes, then what? If not, then surely we would be the laughing stock of the school. Much more important than my momentary infatuation with a boy whom I had not met face to face so far, let alone speak to him, was my secret dream of becoming a doctor which would have to be sacrificed if I were to heed the emotional call of an itinerant preacher. The exchange somehow did not seem worthwhile. So I decided to move away from the group which was contemplating a walk to the pulpit en masse on the last evening of the evangelical campaign. The evening before his last service when he would expect many youngsters to dedicate their lives to the service of the church, those of us who had shown great enthusiasm about the prospect initially, met for a last consultation and to decide whether or not we would go to the pulpit the next evening to take the pledge.

When the group assembled, before anyone had a chance to say anything, I started to speak. "Look, I don't know about you all but I want to tell you that I will not walk to the pulpit tomorrow night because I am too young still and I want to see a bit of life before renouncing it altogether." There was a stunned silence. The other girls looked at one another, some with relief and some with shock; there was no further discussion after my declaration and one by one the girls left the meeting place. We did go to the next evening's service because not going was not an option for us. But we were all subdued and avoided looking at each other. Even the former vigour of our singing was muted by a nameless presence. While the Reverend droned on, I wondered what my friends thought about my little speech the evening before and why nobody else spoke up. Even as I thought this I knew that as far as I was concerned the debate was over because I had opted for life.

The end of the evangelical campaign in our church meant the exit of Rev. Sahu from our lives and we reverted to our staid, monotonous routine of school and hostel. But in later years we heard about him becoming a very famous preacher who brought many converts to the fold of various churches in the region. If his brief sojourn in our church left any permanent impressions on the congregation, especially young people like us, it was difficult to see, because nothing seemed to have changed in our humdrum existence in the boarding school. Though we did not exactly understand the contents of his sermons, the vigour of his convictions and his persuasive oratory had us swaying for a while, like a burst of strong wind overtaking tired travellers on a dusty road who wonder afterwards what had happened. But how quickly the dust settled again as if their journey had never been interrupted by anything. Was the storm real or was the visitation only a fleeting day-dream?

Smugglers

Though a residential school, there were quite a number of day-scholars who came from the town. Our contact with them were strictly monitored so that they could not bring in any material to the school except their books. During the tiffin break they sat around the compound eating their food while we trooped back to the hostel for our measly tiffin. And after school, we went our different ways: they to their homes and we to our hostel.

But even such rigorous precautions could not prevent the occasional breach like the time when a classmate brought in

a book with pornographic sketches of nude bodies, both male
and female. It also had instructions about sexual intercourse.
But I never actually got to see it because after a rapid round
of selected girls the day-scholar prudently whisked it away
from the school. I came to know about it only afterwards
when the fortunate girls who handled the book began to use
some new vocabulary on the sly and began having fun about
their secret lore. Though I eventually came to know the
identity of the smuggler, it never occurred to me to play the
snitch and inform on her, though I did feel left out.

On another occasion a book of a different kind was being
whispered about among the senior girls. It was most probably
around 1956 or '57 when the Naga insurgency movement
had started in right earnest and was causing a tremendous
upheaval in the region. It seems that an enterprising
writer came out with a novel about it where a person was
captured by the rebels and how he eventually escaped to tell
the story. The book was in Assamese and was called *Noga
Bidruhir Hatot;* roughly translated it means *In the Hands of
Naga Rebels.* The few who got the chance to read portions
of it spoke of the 'heroism' of the rebels. This time round
too, the book vanished before I could even look at the cover.
But what was said about the rebels sent me into a period
of fantasy: I would run away from the hostel and join the
movement and become a 'heroine' myself! But of course like
all fanciful hysteria, this one also soon died a natural death
from the burden of studies and menial work in the hostel.

But there was an occasion when I was caught in a sticky
situation about another smuggled item: a love letter. One of
my classmates was, according to her, in love with a much
older man who had just joined as a junior engineer in her
hometown. On one occasion she told me that once he had
even kissed her! I dismissed her claim saying that she was
making it all up. She retorted angrily and told me that she

would one day show me evidence to prove that she was telling the truth. I did not realize to what extent a love-crazed person could go to prove her claim but she kept her promise and that is how I was caught in the biggest crisis of my life in the hostel.

One day, during recess, she asked me to come to her House because she had something important to show me. When we entered the dorm, there was nobody, so she quickly stood on her bed and yanking open her trunk on the shelf above, showed me a letter from her boyfriend dated ten days ago in which he poured out his love for her. I was shocked; by the letter of course but also the nonchalant way she kept it in the folds of her skirt. She told me that a classmate posted her letters to him and her letters too came on that girl's address. After I read it, she looked at my terror-stricken face and demanded, "Now do you believe me?" I nodded and ran to my House to eat my tiffin and then went back to school. All the way back to school my mind was reeling; I had become an accomplice in her crime of receiving and posting letters through a day-scholar by reading it. She had broken a cardinal rule of the school for which dishonourable expulsion would be the inevitable outcome both for her as well as the girl from town. That I had read the letter and not reported to the Super would make me equally guilty if it was known that I had done so and I too would suffer the same fate.

Just as I had feared, unbeknown to us, another hosteller had seen us standing on the bed and reading the letter and she reported the matter to the Matron who in turn told the Super. By the time school was over, the matter had become official knowledge. My nightmare had begun. The Super sent for me in the evening and demanded to know what I was doing in that House during recess. I said I had gone there to look at my friend's new blouse, which was fortunately true.

She had a lovely new blouse she had not yet worn. She asked me whether I had seen any letter, I said 'no' with a straight face. The Super threatened me saying that if I was lying, I would be expelled along with her. But I stuck to my denial and eventually she had to let me go because there was no concrete evidence against me.

Luckily for the day-scholar, every time my friend received a letter she would destroy the envelope and when grilled about the confiscated letter my classmate said that someone threw it at her during a Saturday outing through town. The signature of the boy was illegible and her name also was not written anywhere except the word 'darling' on top of the letter. It could not be proved beyond doubt that it was addressed to her. But all the same it was found in her trunk and therefore she had to bear the consequences.

She was worried stiff that I would divulge the means through which she received her letters and wanted to ask me to keep her secret. But it would be imprudent for her to be seen with me, so she sent a couple of her House-mates to request me not to say anything. I was in the meantime beginning to feel a perverse sense of power in thinking how easily I could ruin her future by snitching on her. But instantly I reminded myself that doing that would mean doom for me as well. So I gallantly assured the emissaries to tell her that I'd rather die before I divulged her secret to anyone.

In the end neither my friend nor myself was questioned further and I did not know how this episode of the smuggled letter was resolved. But, for me, another loyalist was added to the roster of my followers! As for my relationship with the Super was concerned, it became worse as she had one more grudge to hold against me and I knew that she would never let slip an opportunity to extract her revenge on me.

Asian Flu

That opportunity presented itself sooner than either of us expected. It came in the form of the Asian flu of 1957 which was raging through the Asian countries; hence the label. There were reports of people dying of this even in our town and several day-scholars were also reported to be afflicted by it. There was quite a bit of panic in the hostel also because a few girls had become sick and were isolated in the school infirmary. As a precautionary measure, all the other hostellers were required to gargle with saline water twice a day: once before going to school and the second time after school. They had to do it standing outside their Houses so that the Matron could monitor them. I do not know how effective this was but it was made compulsory and as usual we were told that defaulters would be 'punished'.

Being the Mahi of 3rd House, it was my responsibility to ensure that every single girl under my charge should comply with the rules about gargling in this manner. In the beginning we all dutifully did what was demanded of us. But gradually we found that we could not spare the precious minutes doing this which would mean that we could either not finish our maths homework or would have to forfeit our bath. The number of girls standing in front of the 3rd House gargling away became fewer and fewer and one day there was nobody standing there going through the ritual. This was noticed by the Matron and duly reported to the Super.

She was waiting for me at the gate of the hostel as I made my weary way home carrying a load of homework to be finished by the evening before lights-out. She asked me why our House did not obey the rule about gargling; I replied that due to heavy homework we missed it in the morning but were going to do it in the evening. I said 'sorry' to her on behalf of all in our House and promised never to fail in the future. This did not cut any ice with her. She asked if we were the only ones with heavy homework; and added that if the others could find time, how come it was only us who found it difficult to follow the rule?

She then picked a few of us and ordered us to clean the surroundings of the infirmary every day after school, beginning on that very day. Of course we had to do as she ordered. After three days of this labour one of the girls, a student of class VI fell ill and had to be brought to the infirmary with high fever. We all looked at each other when we came to know about this after school. Of course we could do nothing but continue with this punishment labour until, one by one, all of us contracted the flu and were admitted to the infirmary.

Even now as I recall the nature of the headaches that assaulted me during the bouts of fever, I shudder with an inner rage at the inhuman treatment meted out to us by the revengeful Super. During these bouts I would tie a string round my head because I feared that my head would break into splinters, so severe was the pain. Tears would roll down my eyes and I would grit my teeth so as to stifle the sobs that racked my body. I do not remember how many days I was laid up with this dreaded flu because I seemed to have lost all track of time.

By then the infirmary was full of sick girls, each undergoing the same pain and agony but my pain was somewhat more sinister because I believed that the Super deliberately exposed us to the infection by making us work in close proximity with sick girls and thus making us more vulnerable to the disease. If my days were plagued by fever and pain, my nights were haunted by a strange dream. Almost on a regular basis I would dream that I was in a tube-like contraption which was being pulled up by a thin string while wild creatures swirled and growled as if to devour me.

In the dream, I would try to scream but no sound came out of my throat; instead, I felt as if I could not breathe and was left with a violent constriction of my heart. At this point I would wake up with a start to find myself sweating profusely and gasping for air. These dreams occurred even during daytime and the nurse told me that my body went into terrible contortions several times a day.

There were times during this confinement when I thought that I was going to die, especially after the strange dreams. But funnily enough I do not remember any fear or panic at the prospect: only an enormous rage at the Super for inflicting this pain and keeping me away from school for so many days. I would worry about not doing well in the forthcoming terminal examination. And these thoughts perhaps helped me to bear the pain and kept me from worrying too much about dying.

Some of the patients who were there when we were admitted were released and gradually only a few of us remained. I was told by the nurse that the Super visited us every night to ask about our condition and said that she was particularly worried about me. I kept quiet and as I regained my strength and could stay awake much longer without pain, I dreaded the prospect of the Super finding me awake when she came round, so I resolved to be on my guard. I was determined not to speak to her ever again, so great was my anger.

As I had feared one early evening she came and entered the infirmary. As soon as I heard her voice I tied the string I had kept under my pillow round my head and slipped into bed. Turning my face towards the wall, I pretended to be asleep. She came to my bed and stood there without saying anything. She knew that I was not asleep because the nurse must have told her that I had no fever and was well on my way to recovery. And also that only a few minutes ago I was

telling jokes and we were having a good time. I could sense
her standing there mute for quite sometime, and I wanted
her to know that I would reject all her overtures showing her
concern. I couldn't care less that my attitude might hurt her
and remained stiff until I heard the door close behind her
retreating steps. She did not respond when the nurse called
out, "Good night, Missba".

From that time onwards the Super truly became a figure
of menace to me and I developed perhaps an unreasonable
resentment against her. We were discharged from the
infirmary and soon resumed our classes. But I was a different
person now; if in the past I had quibbles with the Super, once
it was over I forgot about the whole thing. But now I was
determined to show her my anger and resentment in every
possible way.

Football Tournament

Soon after this episode, the town was agog with an important
event: the prestigious State Football Tournament was taking
place in the local playground where the team from Nagaland
was steadily progressing to the finals. In an unprecedented
move, the Super was allowing the high school girls to go and
watch the games in batches because of some holidays we
had. By the time we were discharged from the Infirmary
after our bout with flu, the semi-final day had arrived and we
decided to seek permission to accompany the day's group.
The Super refused to allow our group to go saying that we
had disobeyed her and therefore forfeited the privilege. We
were stunned by her statement and stood speechless for
quite sometime. Everyone was looking at me and urging me
to argue with her. I did not know what to say, but at the
same time an insane rage was building up in me. She had
made us contract the flu on account of the nature of her

punishment; she had seen how much we had suffered and yet again she was trying to inflict another punishment on us by denying a privilege accorded to all the others. It was a 'double' punishment!

Resolving to try once more to plead with her, I stepped forward and said, "Missba, we request you to forgive us for what happened. And we have already been punished for that; you saw how much we suffered, how sick we have been." She did not respond immediately but looked at us with hard, unrelenting eyes. She kept her eyes longest on me and said, "No, I cannot let you go, your behaviour has been unforgivable."

When I heard these words, I lost all control and taking a step forward, shouted at her, "What kind of missionary are you if you say that you cannot forgive? You cannot punish us twice for the same thing. You may be white outside, but you are all black inside because your mind is evil". Saying this, I herded our group back to the hostel, convinced that whatever chance we had of pleading our way to the match, it was surely over after my angry outburst.

But we were in for a big surprise. After an hour or so, the Matron came looking for me and said that the Super had changed her mind and would allow our group to go for the match in town. I did not know what to say to her. She told me to call the others and be ready within twenty minutes. But before she went to her quarters to get ready to accompany us, she said something strange to me, "You know you made Missba cry today? Your words were really cruel." I did not know what to make of this statement; I only knew that my head was still reeling with the suddenness of the happenings and my spontaneous outburst. So I simply turned away from her to inform the others and get ready for the hard-earned outing.

But I remember that we did not enjoy the match at all;

in fact we were happy when it was over. We walked back to the hostel with moody faces and troubled minds, though we had earlier celebrated our 'victory' over the Super when we learnt that we would be allowed to go. But at the end of it all, there was only bitterness in my mind, against whom, I was not sure at all. Slowly a realization was beginning to dawn on me that life was more than winning petty 'victories' over real or imagined enemies.

Perhaps it was the moment when I began to grow out of my adolescent anger against the world for seeming to be so unfair to me.

Bound by Hubert

This episode is one of a kind in the list of my misadventures in school. It happened when I was in class VI. It relates to the 'binding' of a tattered hymn book by a boy called Hubert who lived close to our hostel. I was not aware that such a service could be availed because he was a boy and we were not supposed to have any contact with boys, even those who belonged to our church. Secondly, I did not know him at all. All that I knew was that several girls had their hymn books repaired and re-bound by this boy.

When I saw the new-looking hymn books, I said I also wanted my hymn book made new. One girl said that she'd arrange it but I had to pay a rupee for it and more importantly never take her name if anything happened. I agreed and shelled out the precious rupee from my meagre pocket money. Within the week the hymn book came back to me looking almost new. I was truly overcome by the novelty of the 'new' look and wrote on the front page, *Bound by Hubert!* I was very proud of my new hymn book.

But my euphoria did not last long because one evening I was sent for by the Super with the instruction that I should bring my hymn book along. I knew I was in trouble but there was neither time to erase what I had written on the book nor any way to make it look old again. So, holding the book I made my way to the bungalow. I was admitted and made to sit on the floor which was the designated place for us when we were summoned in her presence. She began grilling me about the book, how I had it done, who had helped me and lastly how many times I met this boy. I did not respond to any of these questions, I kept my head bowed down and remained in one position for nearly an hour. Getting no response from me, the Super confiscated my book and said that I would be punished for what I did.

It amuses me even now to think about the punishment: I would not be allowed to accompany the others to Wednesday evening services for a month and would have to spend the hour sitting on the floor in her bungalow reading chapters from the Bible that she would choose! At that time I resented only the boredom of that solitary hour in reading obscure prophets from the Old Testament which made no impact on me at all. In fact, I only pretended to read while my mind was elsewhere. I am recording this episode in order to understand the rationale behind this particular 'punishment' which still eludes me.

The very instrument of the so-called 'punishments' meted out in the school and hostel, though meant as deterrents, never seemed to have achieved their goal. The sad part is that while some were made victims of this on the slightest pretext, there was no attempt at determining why these girls were reacting to the system more negatively than others. It was more like a surface treatment of some deep-seated malady of the unfortunate few. No words of counselling ever followed the physical punishment; only another red mark on your rap sheet, waiting for the ultimate day of condemnation. But luckily for me that day never came and I managed to survive through the six years with these occasional encounters with the authorities, especially with the Super in whose book I must have occupied a permanent place as the most likely culprit in every misadventure!

Cold of a Certain Kind

Life in the hostel was tough, to say the least. But it was during winter that another kind of problem beset poor girls like me. The hostel provided hard wooden beds but the girls had to bring their own bedding. My bed did not have any mattress because I or rather my brothers could not afford to buy one. There was only an old blanket which was folded double and over which a thin cotton sheet was spread. A lumpy pillow and a thin quilt completed my bedding. In summer the quilt also went under the sheet. When winter came it was taken out from there to cover me at night. The bed clothes got an airing every weekend when it did not rain. The quilt being stuffed with cotton absorbed the sun's heat on these occasions and on winter nights there is nothing more comforting than to get under such a covering to fight the cold. But the comfort would not last beyond a short period; firstly because the stuffing had formed into individual lumps on account of the cheap and loose stitching and also because it had been slept on during the summer months. So it could not sustain the initial heat still trapped in the cotton. The quilt itself now became the repository of the winter cold permeating the night.

Winters in the plains can be devastatingly cold and on many such nights the natural cold of winter and the quilt-cold seeped through to my body and settled mostly on my back. While shivering under the lumpy quilt and trying to maintain a steady body posture, I used to promise myself that one day I would buy myself the thickest, fluffiest and softest quilt in the world which would resist and keep out all the cold of the wintery earth which seemed to have lodged permanently on my back. The memory of those cold-induced sleepless nights still haunts me on certain dismal days of winter even though I may be sitting in front of a roaring fire all bundled up in winter clothing.

Cheese Thieves

The matriculation examinations used to be in the month of April and by that time the hostel would be full with the other regular students. The matric girls were required to be in the hostel from the beginning of the new session so that we could study properly under the supervision of our teachers. But since the Houses were occupied by the regular hostellers, we were housed in a small cottage within the hostel compound. As we did not have to attend classes, we were assigned to assist the Matron in distributing snacks for tiffin and also in distributing the rations to each House for the day's meals. It was the tiffin items which tempted us to become thieves.

The hostel used to get some imported food items like cheese and egg powder which could be fried up like omelettes. The cheese used to come in round tins and the whole chunk would be lifted after the lid was cut off. Then the chunk would be sliced into equal pieces to be distributed with a rusk (kata biscuit) to each girl. Since no one could determine exactly how many pieces the lump of cheese could be cut into, we sneaked big chunks of it in the fold of our saris along with the biscuits and munched to our hearts' content in the privacy of our little cottage!

For me there was another bonus; some of the girls did not like cheese and they would throw their share away. When I learnt this, I spread the word that I would be happy to receive their share. So the last three months of my stay in the hostel was a veritable feast of cheese!

Certain Other Lessons

It was a tradition with the Principal that she would invite the class X students of the hostel in batches to her bungalow for dinner. At these dinners she would teach us how to lay the table, place the cutlery in the appropriate place and how to serve the food. Initially, to me, the whole exercise appeared to be farcical and contradictory. Here we were, being introduced to aspects of an incongruous and alien life-style while we lived the way that we did in the hostel! How was laying a perfect dining table relevant to us? How did it matter at all? But what I could not see at that point of time was that her vision for us had already stretched beyond the limits of this hostel and that she was allowing us some glimpses of a finer world waiting for us out there.

For our batch the Principal had made a pumpkin pie as dessert. Though I do not recall what the other dishes tasted like, the dessert was delicious. It was also a revelation about the potential of this humble vegetable, and how it could be converted in to such a delicacy. I have tried my hand at this dish, but I am sorry to admit that so far, I have not succeeded in turning out anything even remotely resembling the marvel that I had the good fortune to eat that evening so, so long ago!

It was also the evening when I committed the dumbest and biggest 'faux pax' of my life. After dinner the Principal said that we were going to play a quiz game and we all sat in a circle on the carpet. She started asking questions like 'what is the shortest verse in the Bible?' (Jesus wept) and 'who is the shortest man in the Bible?' (Bildad, the Shoehite, one of Job's friends) After a while, she introduced another game: which went like: Match the name of a tree to a part of the body, e.g. a *palm* (tree). A place of worship: *temple* etc. Then came the moment that did me in. The next word she wanted was a denomination of money that matched a part of the body. I thought hard and wanting to score before the others had time to hazard a guess, I shouted pennies. And instantly I knew what I had done and wished that I had kept my stupid mouth shut. The Principal averted her eyes as she mumbled, no, it's *crown*. I wanted to apologize but could not find the words. I wished I could disappear because I believed that I had managed to lose all the goodwill that she had shown me throughout my stay in the school by uttering that word in a moment of extreme vanity.

I like to believe that she must have forgiven my immature utterance because when I got married she sent me a set of silver spoons as a belated wedding gift. However I have to add this though I am not implying anything here; strangely enough there were only five spoons in the packet!

As expected in a Christian school, we had other regular services in the hostel as well as an evening service in the school chapel on Sundays for high school students. Unlike the hostel services, the chapel service was conducted in English where everyone had to take part by turn. They were conducted in all solemnity and seriousness as in the church. Though we went through the motions without giving any serious thought about the implications then, on hindsight I believe that these sessions did a lot to give us confidence when we had to stand before our peers and lead the service or read the Bible or pray, and this experience is something which I value very much. These sessions gave us the courage to stand before a bigger congregation in the church to read Bible verses voluntarily when given the call.

Another course on leadership was the system of selecting 'mahis' every year for each House who acted as a point of liaison with the Matron and the Super. Being responsible for the smooth running of the hostels, these girls, the mahis, learnt how to manage time and human resources and maintain disciple of the group under their supervision. They had to manage each House efficiently; otherwise they would be the first ones to be hauled up if there was any problem. The sense of responsibility thus learnt enhanced our own self-worth.

But above all, the most valuable lesson I learnt in the six years that I spent in this hostel was about human relationships. The hostellers came from many different strata of society; some had rich parents, some were daughters of white tea garden managers born to adivasi women, some were daughters of doctors, preachers and teachers. Each girl came with the culture of her family into the hostel. But here, there was no hierarchy; everybody was treated as equal, no rich, no poor, no high class, no low class. What mattered was how one behaved, followed the discipline of the school and hostel and, more importantly how well one did in studies. By the time I reached High School, and was doing well in studies, much of my inferiority complex was gone. But in a deep recess of my mind there was the inexorable knowledge that I was still a homeless orphan and I had to live with it.

Academic Foundation

The education we received in this school was of such high standard that it became the corner-stone of our future academic careers. The subjects we studied included English, Assamese, History, Geography, Mathematics, Domestic Science, Elementary Science, Commercial Geography (optional, in lieu of Assamese) and additional subjects like Hygiene and Additional Mathematics. Only the marks in excess of the pass marks of thirty in these two subjects were added to the over-all tally in the final Matriculation exam.

The kind of teaching that we were subjected to can best be described as brutally thorough. For example, in the Geography classes, we were supposed to learn everything about a country; its boundaries, both physical and political, with the capital cities, rivers, mountains, railway and road systems, and even the climate and vegetation etc. but on top of that we had to draw the countries and plot these aspects on each different map! I wonder where we found time for other subjects, because things were equally thorough in the other subjects also. History included both British history starting from the Norman conquest up to the establishment of the East India Company and Indian history from the Indus valley civilization, the raids of Genghis Khan up to the last Mughal emperor's incarceration. After that the reign of the different Governor Generals was also included in the syllabus. This is but a small illustration only from a vast and comprehensive curriculum. Even in a subject like the Bible, the teaching was equally thorough. Starting from Genesis, we had to wade through both the Testaments up to Revelations. I remember we even had to study the various routes of St. Paul's last voyages with the help of actual maps!

But it was the writers included in our English papers in high school who opened a whole new universe for me and I can say with absolute conviction now that my love of literature overtook all other interests after I read them.

Needless to say we had excellent teachers who devoted their lives to teaching. In junior school we had a teacher by the name of Miss Norun Sangma who taught us arithmetic. Oh, how we dreaded her classes if we had not done our homework for the day. She would haul defaulters to the front and make them do their sums on the blackboard in front of the whole class and God have mercy on any one who blundered! But her strict discipline made us more careful and hard working. Other teachers like Mrs. Louise Sangma, Miss Lydia Singh, Miss Tara Das, Miss Aruna, Mr. Sen who taught us Mathematics in High School and Miss Robinson, the Super who taught us Domestic Science and Miss Evans, the Principal, who taught us English and Hygiene. Both Miss Robinson and Miss Evans taught us the Bible also.

Managing to tackle all these subjects in school with the meticulous standard required of us and handling the multifarious chores in the hostel taught us the most valuable lesson in life: management of available time. It is this quality which was inculcated into our character that has stood us all in good stead throughout our lives.

Personally, the academic foundations in the various subjects mentioned above have facilitated my passage through the college exams which I took without attending many classes and this is living testimony to the quality of education imparted in this school.

We considered the rules of the school and hostel to be harsh and even cruel at times but they applied equally to all. The inherent justice of the rules acted as the levellers and mediators among us so that no other distinction could be super-imposed on the one identity of all; we were all students of the same school and hostel.

I remember another aspect of our hostel life, the significance of which has struck me only in the course of writing this. There was a system of special friendships between a senior and a junior girl where the senior became the exclusive 'baidew' (elder sister) and the junior the special 'bhonti' (younger sister). Through the pact of 'sisterhood', the younger girl would be at the beck and call of the older, had to do all her bidding and no one else's. The older girl in return would promise to love only the 'bhonti' and would become her 'protector' of sorts. It was some kind of exclusionary practice which kept others out of this particular bond. These relationships were taken very seriously which demanded absolute loyalty from each other. There were many incidents of bickering and even threats to the intruders who were suspected of attempting to break up an established relationship. But when the new 'suitor' was successful, there would be scenes of real tears; some girls went to the extent of saying that they would commit suicide if the relationship was not restored.

I was not aware of this practice when I first came to the hostel. I remember there were some attempts by the senior girls to draw me into such a relationship, not directly but through remarks like 'So and so baidew likes you'. But not knowing what it was all about I merrily ignored the broad hints and perhaps when they realized that I was not at all like any of the junior girls they simply gave up the idea. Anyway I would perhaps not have made a very good or tame 'bhonti'!

When the quarrels and bickering about the 'breach of trust' among the baidews and bhontis became more frequent and open, the Matron and other teachers began to view the system with some alarm. They summoned the known pairs and tried to break up all such relationships with their partners. It was not an easy task because some girls had become too dependant on their baidews and found it difficult to adjust to the more general relationships. But the authorities persisted in trying to discourage these ties and gradually this practice was weeded out completely by the time I was in the senior classes. Any attempt at excluding anyone else from the general bonding within hostel life was viewed with suspicion and the authorities intervened to break up the exclusive pairs. These seemingly small things, I believe, went a long way in teaching us to maintain harmonious personal relationships with everyone in the hostel. I am sure that this healthy attitude has helped us to adjust in the different environments where we eventually found ourselves.

Life has an amazing way of sifting the good from the bad and building foundations on the former. The lessons learnt through the vicissitudes in the hostel have become the strengths of my life and I believe that the same can be said of all the others who have passed through the portals of this excellent school. In so many ways the hostel *was* a 'home' for all of us, though we never thought of it that way then. And it has taken me these fifty odd years to realize this truth.

Life also has its own mysterious ways of guiding and leading you to revelations such as these. At this stage in life, I feel truly privileged to have spent my formative years in an institution like my old school. There is no rancour in recalling the hardships that we underwent, but only a sense of wonder that we survived those trials. I can also say with absolute confidence that the lessons we learnt from our experiences trained us to face greater trials in life and to overcome them.

The Last Days

As I mentioned earlier, by the time a batch acquired the status of 'matric students', they were treated with some sense of awe as well as diffidence: they had reached an important milestone. These students were somehow excluded from the normal routine of the school and hostel: they did not have to attend classes and were not required to participate in the running of the hostel. The matric exams were held in April by which time the regular school routine which started in January, would be in full swing. That meant that there was already a Xth class. We were therefore in a sense 'redundant' or 'super numerary' for a few months before the exams. It meant that we could not be kept in the Houses as regular hostellers. So we were kept in a small cottage away from the big Houses though we were assigned to eat in designated hostels. Our time, the entire days leading to the exams were devoted to revising the lessons we'd learned earlier. Whereas during our days as regular hostellers, lessons had to be adjusted with military precision with the other duties of the hostel; now there was a new sense of freedom from other chores and our time was at our disposal. We all savoured this new-found status!

The last days of my stay in the hostel now appear to me like a fast-moving montage: being cooped up in a small room with many others, everyone trying to cram last minute information into an already over-burdened brain. We counted the number of days available to us to do the revision and allot equal number of days to the subjects. It had all to be done in time for the exams. We would walk to the town High School where the Matriculation exams were being held and would walk back to the hostel tired and hungry. Sometimes to our delight there would be some cold rice and dal waiting for us but there was still no afternoon tea.

Before going to study for the next exam, there would be discussions on the day's performance. No one dared ask the others directly how they fared, the comments would be non-committal and would only be on the 'toughness' or otherwise of the day's question paper. If a girl thought she did particularly badly, the only sign would be a hurriedly wiped teardrop. Each matric batch had a double burden for our school had a long history of excellence: year after year our school boasted of 100% pass records in the Matric exams, with many Distinctions (80% and above) in various subjects. Therefore no batch wanted to be remembered as the one which produced failures and strangely that dread was as heavy as the one about our own personal performance. But inwardly we entertained a certain confidence because of the excellent grooming that we had in high school, which was further enhanced by the extra efforts put in for the last few months. We believed that we were ready to face the most crucial test of our lives and would succeed. And so on every exam day we marched to the exam hall with new hope of doing better than what we had done so far in school.

To be honest, I do not remember clearly the details of the very last day when I left the hostel for good; how I packed my few belongings into the battered tin trunk I had carried to this school from my old home. I also do not recall any specific goodbyes to my classmates, I only remember that my eldest brother was waiting for me outside the main gate with my bhabi and they had managed to bring a jeep. Everything seemed to have happened so fast: one minute I was inside the hostel saying good bye to those of my classmates who were still around, and the next, sitting in the back seat of the jeep going towards a future about which I had not the faintest idea. Once again I began to feel displaced and disoriented. One thing I was sure of: that an important phase of my life was over. As I left the familiar confines of the hostel on that day, little did I know that my life would be launched into a totally uncharted territory: I would be married off within a month of my matric exams, even before the results were declared. Compelled by forces way beyond my comprehension, I was forced to accept my fate with nothing in my arsenal except the strengths I developed in this school, the only 'home' I'd known these last six years.

PART III

Married Life: Plunge into the Unknown

That day when I left the hostel for the last time with my brother and bhabi, I did not have the vaguest idea about my future. For the moment, there was a sort of relief and jubilation that I had crossed an important milestone and was free of the restricting confines of the hostel. It was only when the family began to talk openly about a marriage and I realized that it was *my* marriage they were talking about, that I began to feel apprehensive. Once again it reminded me that I was without a proper location for myself. I resisted the idea as best as I could by saying that I wanted to pursue higher studies and did not want to get married yet. But the family told me categorically that I was being unrealistic because no one in the family was in a position to finance my studies. Ultimately the overwhelming pressure from family, especially my maternal grandmother, proved too much for me to withstand. Besides, the more they talked, the clearer it became to me also how hopeless my future was. Once again the old feeling of being 'homeless' began to overwhelm me and I finally gave in, consoling myself that I would at least have a 'home' of my own at last. I even allowed myself to be caught in the frenzy of the hectic preparations; hectic it was because there was hardly a month to the big day after my return to the hills. The marriage itself was the hottest item of gossip in town because the groom came from a prominent family, well-to-do and boasting of siblings who held important government jobs. The townspeople were caught by surprise when they learnt who the bride

was going to be: an obscure, unheard-of girl barely out of
boarding school, with no parents and her siblings too of no
consequence. Only the eldest brother had just qualified for
a gazetted post a month ago. There was no wealth to speak
of as far as the girl was concerned. On top of that, she was
gawky, unsophisticated and ill at ease in the genteel society
the groom's family moved in.

How then did the match happen? It was an open secret
that it was the groom's family that asked for my hand and
insisted on the early marriage. There were also whispers
that the parents were desperate to separate their son from
his liaison with a beautiful socialite who had gone to college
in Shillong and was determined to marry into the family.
Some went to the extent of saying that the groom's mother
had once turned her out of the house because she was
brazenly visiting her son too frequently. Normally a girl
never goes to a boyfriend's house uninvited by the family
and even when she did, she would have to be chaperoned
by a cousin or an aunt. The groom's friends too were teasing
him for agreeing to marry this 'village' girl when he'd had
quite a few 'town' girlfriends to choose from. According to
them, I was all wrong for him, did not dress in frock and
skirt, still wore a sari or mekhela sador, had never used any
make-up and worst of all sported my long hair in a braid! No
bobbed hair, no lipstick, no modern clothes, *'Ye kahase utha
ke laya re tu?'* one non-local friend quipped. Of course I was
not aware of any of these comments until much later after
the marriage. Even his brother, I was later told, asked him
in disbelief when I was first presented to the family, 'You're
really going to marry this – girl?' Incidentally, he was the
first 'sahib' in the family.

In other circles however, people were talking
knowledgeably about the reason why the father's choice
fell on me when there were many smarter girls who could

have easily fitted into their social level. Even the current 'girlfriend' would have fitted the bill, except for some 'reputation' she had earned during her college days. But the more important reason for rejecting her was the fact that though she belonged to the same village, she came from a minor clan. They nodded their wise heads and said that he was right in choosing a girl from the founding clan of the same village. For him, it appeared that my family's impoverished state did not matter because he had enough. What mattered to him was that he would be forging an alliance for his kith and kin in the village which would guarantee the support of the founding clan. In all fairness, it must be added here that my clan also welcomed the alliance not only because my future was being taken care of, but because of a long-standing tradition of alliances between our two clans, which they claimed always prospered and produced many children! My maternal grandmother was almost ecstatic when she heard of my impending marriage because she said that my mother, if she was alive, would have been very happy because I was getting married to a man from her (mother's) clan! Except for the flippant remarks and cynicism of the town's modern set, it appeared that on the whole, the forthcoming marriage was seen to be a good thing for both families.

As for me I did not have the faintest idea of what marriage entailed. Even the date was unknown to me until a cousin wanted confirmation. "So," he remarked, "you're getting married on the 22nd?" I was taken aback, 22nd of May was just three weeks away and a little over a month after my exams and no one had consulted or told me about any date. I challenged him, "Who told you?" At this, he burst out laughing, "Everybody knows it, where have you been?" Indeed, where I had been was difficult to explain; he would not understand if I told him that I was gleefully building a fantasy-land of happily ever-afters and I had already convinced myself that I was really in love with this man though I'd met him only a few times so far and that too in the company of others. He was much older than me but I have to admit that I thought he was handsome, he wore natty clothes and when he spoke, his voice sounded gentle and nice. He had also built a successful business. Besides he drove a smart Willis jeep! Above all, I also believed that he did 'want' to marry me and being wanted by someone was a new and novel sensation. Never having had any opportunity of mixing with boys my own age and never knowing what a relationship with the opposite sex was supposed to be like, I was completely bowled over and all these factors acted as powerful aphrodisiacs for an impoverished girl who had spent all her life longing for love and security. Besides, one was supposed to 'love' one's husband, right? I began to believe that I was indeed, as everyone in my family kept on saying, lucky to have caught the fancy of this influential family and to be marrying such a handsome man!

More novelties were in store for me: my wedding dress was ordered from Mohni Store in Shillong. It was made of thin and transparent white organdie with embossed floral designs to be worn above a flouncy chemise of exquisite satin! The V-shaped neck displayed a long row of pearl buttons, the tapering sleeves ending in an inverted V beyond the wrist. The veil too was white, some net-like material flowing below the waist; that end displaying similar floral designs. A cute pair of white gloves and white suede shoes completed the outfit. When I first saw the ensemble, I hid my face in my hands with disbelief and dismay. Dismay because I thought I could never carry it off and the shoes, I asked myself, how could I wear those heels when most of my growing years I'd gone barefoot? But the oohs and aahs of assorted cousins and aunts prevented me from expressing such self-demeaning thoughts aloud. And I did wear them on my wedding day without disgracing myself, as the few photographs of that day will testify. I still have that dress today with the 22" waistline! Our wedding was touted as the most ostentatious and celebrated wedding of the town, with cakes and pastries also 'imported' from Shillong. After the festivities were over, we moved into a brand new house in father-in-law's compound which had been kept in readiness for us. With such romantic preliminaries, the story of the newly-weds should have surely led to a happily-ever-after but if truth be told, neither of us was truly prepared for the task. The physical structure of the 'home' I'd longed for so much was at my disposal but transforming that dream into reality would take us both into a maze that left us lost and bruised for life.

The Housewife

I never realized how un-ready and incompetent I was in managing a household of two until I tried my hand at housekeeping. I did not know enough cooking, how to go shopping, preparing a menu and above all how to cope with a man both in bed and in the house and in society at large. It was all so bewildering and I could get no help from my mother-in-law or sisters-in-law because our tradition demands that all newly-weds have to fend for themselves from the very first day. Husbands leave their wives alone in these matters because they feel that these are not men's concerns. The worst handicap was that I did not know anything about this man who had become my husband; his likes and dislikes. My past had never prepared me for any predicament like this. There was no mother to guide me, nor any aunt or elderly relative nearby who would give me a tip or two. When I burned the rice or botched up the curry with too much salt in half-cooked meat, it was the silent stare of the man which devastated me because it told me how disappointed he was at my ineptness. Here I was, so eager to please him and make him happy; instead my efforts were turning out to be just the opposite. Those initial months of married life were terribly frustrating and mortifying but I vowed to myself that I would learn to be a better cook, a better 'wife' and better manager of the household. And gradually, with tips from friends and cousins to whom I went for advice in desperation, I did begin to improve my housekeeping skills. Through habit inculcated in boarding life, I maintained the house and surroundings meticulously clean and tidy even if I could not serve a decent meal for quite sometime.

Housekeeping however, is only a physical activity which gets done quickly if you follow a set routine and instruct the helpers properly. Besides that, there was nothing exciting for me to look forward to the whole day. To my dismay I discovered that my husband was not interested in books or music or films and there seemed to be nothing of mutual interest that could draw us out, bring us together in stimulating conversation helping us to know each other better. At the same time I could not participate in any of the activities he was interested in: sitting down with his cronies, playing cards, drinking and endlessly talking about business. The only recourse left for me was to turn to books, my favourite pastime. But living in a town like Mokokchung in the early sixties when there was not a single book-store or library, I was hard-pressed to borrow books from whoever had private collections. In my father-in-law's house also there was an assortment of varied books which came to my rescue. When I came across an old copy of *Readers' Digest*, I began subscribing to it. At some stage they brought out volumes containing works by famous writers and I ordered these Condensed Books. Old copies of *Time* and *Life* from the old house were read and re-read because they carried interesting pictures of celebrities and royalty. I even began to read the sheets of newspapers which were used as wrappings for our purchases. I remember an occasion when I was cooking rice in an aluminium pot over wood fire, at the same time reading a Perry Mason thriller. I was so engrossed in the book that I did not know when the rice was done; only when the strong fire burned through the pot and the smoke and stench of burning rice and aluminium filled the kitchen, I became aware of what happened. The entire pot had to be thrown out and I had to cook another pot of rice. Luckily for me, my husband was not at home but he did come to know about it through the servant. He did not mention it ever, though I wish he had because I felt that his silence was a stronger reproof than a verbal caution which connects the speaker to the listener and things are out in the open between the two.

Evening College

The year I got married, there was great excitement in town because a group of educated young people fresh out of university had got together and decided to open an evening college for employed people and young men and women who could not go elsewhere for further studies. As soon as I heard about it, I pleaded with my husband to allow me to join. At first he was a bit reluctant, how would I walk home after classes in the dark? But I assured him that that a neighbour who was a clerk in an office would also be joining and we would be together. So finally he gave in and I was ecstatic at this unthought-of good fortune of going to college! Classes were held from 4pm onwards in the High School premises and we were truly grateful to these young visionaries who were helping us to improve our lives. In the beginning there were no regular lecturers, the organizers were teaching their subjects like History, English, Civics and Commercial Geography. The students were a motley group: most were married and of varying ages; there were youngsters like me and in the same class there were veteran teachers whom we called uncle or aunty! The atmosphere was most informal because even the organizer/teachers had at one time been students of these old teachers. Some of these older students made it very clear to their 'teachers' that since they were addicted to eating paan, they should not mind if they ate some during the class sometimes! What could the young 'teachers' say?

I enjoyed going to classes and before going made sure that dinner was prepared and the household chores were all done. I started looking for text books, even tattered ones so that I did not miss out in any subject. I truly believed that it was a god-sent opportunity for me to obtain a college education. But the idyllic state did not last long. About a month after I started attending classes, one evening as I was preparing to go to college, I was summoned to the big house. To my surprise it was a full family meeting which included my husband also. I was startled to see him there because I'd thought that he had gone out. My father-in-law began the proceedings by asking where I was going. I said, college; what college, he asked though he knew very well what I was talking about because I knew that a prospective son-in-law, one of the temporary teachers who taught us History had told his fiancé. Then he asked who gave permission for me to join college. I said my husband. Then he began to berate me for not getting his permission too. He began to scold my husband also for not consulting him before saying yes to me. This upset me and I made the mistake of replying that I thought my husband's permission was enough. That set everyone off: about the shame I brought to the family because their daughter-in-law was going out at night with all kinds of people. I looked at my husband for support but he kept quiet all the while and I realized that he was cowed down by their collective rage at what they presumed to be my defiance of their authority. I was stunned at this unfair accusation and felt terribly let down by my husband. When they had spent their energy by taking out their ire at my perceived audacity, I left the big house and went home. I stopped going to college from that time on and that was the end of my college career.

But this humiliating experience did not have the desired effect on me; I refused to be intimidated by their criticism because I was confident that I had not done anything wrong. Instead, a dormant aspect of my personality seemed to have been awakened which resolved to fight for justice for myself. The insinuating accusation had stung me to the core and my husband's failure to speak up for me opened my eyes to an inherent weakness in him. The image that I had harboured about him in my imagination seemed to diminish somewhat. Yet I told myself that he could not have mounted an open rebellion against his own father, who was held in awe by all the children. I could not yet define what I felt exactly but of one thing I was confident: I would never give in meekly to such blatant attempt at unjust subjugation. This incident also re-kindled in my mind the not-so-long-ago flares of resentment against seemingly unjust treatment that I had been subjected to in school and began I wondering if my new life was heading not towards my dreamt of happily-ever-after, but somewhere else. But my desire to be a good wife remained ever strong and I tried to put this incident behind me.

Further studies, at that juncture had to be kept in abeyance and I turned to books once more to keep my mind occupied and stimulated. I also renewed my interest in sewing and began experimenting in turning out tops for myself on the machine. I watched the women in church, mainly their attire and decided to shed my old look. I took to wearing Naga skirts and blouses though the sador was not discarded until much later. On shopping trips, I bought lipstick, eyebrow pencil and nail polish too. When I tried them on and looked in the mirror, I saw a different 'me'! People began to remark on this, especially my sisters-in-law, but by then I did not care any more what they or any one else thought. By then I was a regular subscriber of women's magazines like *Eve's Weekly* and later *Femina* and film magazines too. In short I was slowly becoming aware of myself as a 'woman'; no longer a starry-eyed teenager; though ironically, I was experimenting with maturity not as a giggly teenager but as a married woman still in her teens.

'Growing up' within the conventional mores of marriage was not easy. There were so many taboos regarding what a married woman should or should not do: be reserved with boys, never shout or laugh loudly in the presence of elders, do not answer back to your husband even if you think he is wrong etc, etc. So I tried growing up within these parameters, though when it came to discussing books, music or films, I could do it only with people with similar interest and mostly people of my age, who were friends of my youngest brother-in-law who, incidentally, is older to me by two years. These boys were in college and when they visited my brother-in-law during vacations, they would invariably drift to our house for endless cups of tea and chatter. I felt more alive in their presence which did not go down well with my husband and his family. It was another black mark against me; what they did not realize was that I needed such intellectual stimuli which kept that part of my life awake and alive. This tendency too was viewed as 'pretension'. So early on I learned to develop this dual personality: the meek, docile wife and housewife and the curious, eager person thirsting for more knowledge through books and discussions with like-minded people. Now as I look back on this dichotomy I believe that my hankering after more from life other than what my marriage afforded at that time propelled me to strike out on my own through further studies and launched me on a course that was beset with hard work, loneliness and castigation of the worst sort. This inborn propensity also widened the disenchantment between me and my husband which led us further away from each other over the years to a stage where no rapprochement could save our marriage. It would however be wrong to say that there were no other factors which contributed to the break-down; in all honesty I cannot claim that I was the 'victim' and he the 'guilty' one. Suffice it to say that in the course of the years both of us became 'victims' of our incompatible personalities and equally responsible for the disaster that ripped the family apart.

In retrospect what I can now see is that naively I clung to my romantic notion of love and marriage far too long. I failed to recognize that from the very beginning, love had no place in the union, no matter how much I tried to convince myself that I loved him and that he too reciprocated that sentiment. There was no open discord, but neither was there any soul in our unions which produced children at regular intervals; a son first and then to the great disappointment of my in-laws, a succession of four girls. Outwardly, the family was growing, the business somehow surviving and then came a day when people began to talk of the impending bye-election for the town constituency after the death of the sitting member. A group of businessmen got together and suggested that my husband enter the fray as an independent candidate.

A New Identity

But much before that event, there were some changes in my personal life which need to be noted here because they were to influence the course of my future. Soon after I got married, the Deputy Commissioner's wife mobilized public opinion and persuaded the townspeople to establish an English medium school for the children of officers and citizens of the town. It was called The Town English Kindergarten School and employed a number of educated young girls and boys. When the Management sent an invitation for me to join, I had to have the appointment approved by my father-in-law. So I had my first job, earning the princely sum of Rs.150/ per month! My cousin sister was also a teacher and she was going to appear in the Intermediate Arts Examination of Gauhati University. There was no problem for her because she was single and going to the evening college. Hearing her talk about the forthcoming exam all my old longing for further studies surfaced again and I began to think, would it be possible for me to appear as a private candidate? I knew that I would never be able to write the exam as a regular one because I'd left the college quite a long time ago. The date for sending application forms was fast approaching and my chances of doing the exam seemed remote. Besides these, my biggest hurdle would be the courses, what they had covered in the two years even if the others matters were taken care of. At that time the university did not allow just any non-collegiate student to write the exam as a private candidate.

And then out of the blue, an unexpected opportunity appeared in the person of a family friend who was very fond of me and treated me like his own sister. His name is Talitemjen Jamir from Ungma village. From the very beginning he must have sensed that I was eager to write the exam and offered to give me a certificate as a teacher-candidate of his school where he was the Head Master! (He later joined the Administration and went on to become an IAS officer and retired as a Secretary and Commissioner in the Nagaland government.) The next day I went to his office and along with the certificate obtained from him, posted my application form to the university and in due course got the admit card. But we had to write the exam in a college at Jorhat in Assam; I was not worried on this count because we would be accommodated in the girls' hostel and my cousin would also be with me.

By the time all the paperwork was finished, it was early February and I began collecting books and notes from everyone who would oblige. I even went to the regular college teachers to seek their advice and help in the form of books and old question papers. One morning I was sitting out in the sun and reading a history book when my brother-in-law, on vacation from his seminary at Yeotmal, asked me what I was reading. When I told him that I was going to write the Intermediate Arts exam in April, he exclaimed, "Are you mad? What are your subjects?" I said "English, Alternative English, History, Civics and Commercial Geography". He was aghast and muttered, "You'll surely fail!" I looked him in the eye and asked, "You want to bet?" and before he could react, I continued, "I'll not only pass but will pass in the first division. What will you give me if I win the bet?" "Anything you want", he replied without hesitation because he thought that there was no way that I could win the bet. It was all done in a jocular manner because he never dreamt that I would be able to cover the courses in so short a time. But I did and not only passed but passed in the first division, to every one's surprise including myself. As soon as the results were declared, I wrote a letter to my hapless brother-in-law in Yeotmal telling him the news. I also included a paper cut-out of my shoe-size, instructing him that he should get me a pair of mauvish, leather high heels from Henry's in Calcutta. And the heels should be two and half inches, I instructed. Bless his soul, the dear brother-in-law on his next holiday brought me the shoes and told me that he would never enter into any kind of wager with me in the future!

From the very outset, this phase of my life seemed to have been played out in disjointed compartments. Take for instance my job in the school. Whenever I became pregnant, in the sixth or seventh month I would put in my resignation and the management would accept it without comment. But two or three months after the child was born, the Chairman would visit me to offer the job again and I would accept their offer gladly because I found that I liked teaching and the time spent in school with children and colleagues was a welcome change from the drab monotony of housekeeping and coping with my own children at home. It is not, I want to emphasize, that I did not enjoy being a mother and housewife. But at the same time I must confess that I was looking for something more beyond the scope of these parameters. I still could not articulate what this was but I believed that there could be more to my life than being just a housewife and a lowly-paid teacher in a kindergarten school. It was therefore inevitable that I would look to further studies as the means to add the extra meaning to my life but it took me another nine years to actually try to accomplish this because some other events intervened and the tenor of our life took on a completely different turn.

Public Life

The fifties and sixties in the Naga Hills were a turbulent period and as a result of the events a new state known as Nagaland came into being in 1963. Legislators had to be elected and through these elections a new culture emerged which created deep divides and turned the traditional way of life into a form of 'modernity' both among the rural and urban population. For us too, our young family was caught in the web; the first election that my husband was drawn into was a bye-election, necessitated because the sitting MLA from the town constituency died. The choice fell on him because he was a 'free' man, he had no government job, had a good family background and was believed to be well-to-do. And suddenly from a placid existence, the campaign took us by storm: he entered the fray as an independent candidate because the ruling party already had a candidate of their own. The house was turned into a free-for-all arena, where all kinds of people came and went at all times of the day and night. All our resources went into feeding and pleasing these so-called supporters and our life turned almost into a circus. Success only made things worse; our life was not our own any more and there was no end to the 'demands' of the so-called 'supporters' as we pawned our souls to the great fraud of our times called electoral politics. This phase continued till the third election when my husband lost because, as they said then, his main agents sabotaged the campaign. It may have been a coincidence only, but the next election was won by one of these agents. All that I have learnt from this surreal scramble for the vote is that this system has an inbuilt hazard that corrodes the very essence of integrity in the human soul in the pursuit of power; equally for those who seek it directly and for those who hang onto the seekers after glory and power for vicarious gains. I still remember these years as the most unsettling ones of our marriage in spite of the social elevation gained by my husband as an elected Member of the Legislative Assembly because all the attendant vacuities associated with the status only estranged us further.

Tragedy

It was during this period that we lost our eldest daughter. She was short of three months from her fifth birthday. It was sudden and devastating. She fell ill with diarrhoea one evening and by the next day she was gone. It was our first experience with death in the family and we were both utterly overwhelmed by the reality: the suddenness of it left us with many unanswered questions. Should we have taken her to the hospital in spite of the fact that his cousin, who was the Civil Surgeon, was treating her at home? Would taking her to the hospital have saved her? We would never know but to this day I carry the burden of guilt as though I failed to assess the gravity of her ailment and let her slip away from life. Had she lived, she would have been 49 years on April 24th 2012. Her name was Sungtiyenla. When another daughter was born to us a year after the tragedy, we gave this name to her and somehow we believed that our lost daughter was with us once more.

After the event I went into a deep depression, resenting everything alive around me. I felt as if a piece of me was buried with her. She died in February, a bleak month; but by March the trees were sending forth new shoots, flowering bushes were budding and even the bird-songs sounded more cheerful. It seemed so unfair that life should go on when hers had been so cruelly snuffed out. I resented the awakening nature which plunged me deeper into sorrow and guilt. I looked at her clothes and shoes and thought it unfair that they should survive while she was no longer there. I wanted to destroy everything that belonged to her so that they would not remind me of her absence. I did not apply for leave from school but stopped going to work; I said, 'Let them sack me, I don't care'. But nothing of that sort happened; instead my colleagues came to visit me regularly and tried to cheer me up. But I refused to get back to normal, thinking it would be so wrong, with her in the cold ground and me continuing to live as if nothing had changed. Then one day a colleague came alone after school and we chatted for quite a while. I could see that she was trying to tell me something but didn't know how to do it. The pauses between our mundane exchanges were becoming longer. Eventually, leaving a big sigh, she said, "Look, this is your first experience with death in the family but I have witnessed the death of my parents and brother, so believe me I know what you are going through. You have mourned long enough now; you have to let go of her spirit so that her soul rests in peace." Her words touched me deeply.

I sat in the gathering darkness of the evening and thought about her words. I then realized that I was mourning as if death and the unfairness of it all had happened only in our family. When I thought about this friend and her cheerfulness, I understood that just as she had done, I had to overcome grief for the dead in order to care for the living; I still had four children to care for, I told myself. And that moment of truth began the process of my recovery from deep depression into the ranks of the living. Death had visited our family and the void would forever remain in our hearts, but we had to let the experience teach us to cherish what we still had.

All throughout these years of political manoeuverings, I continued teaching in the school because it provided me with an opportunity for maintaining a separate identity and also because it was convenient to put the children in the school where I taught. So my school-going routine would include dressing up the two elder ones, giving instructions to the maid for the two who stayed at home, preparing tiffin for the three of us and marching with them uphill to the school in the morning. It was hectic but I enjoyed doing this because I believed it had a 'purpose'. I earned quite a

reputation for being a hard task-master and disciplinarian,
but also as a good teacher. I say this because when I meet
men and women whom I taught in the school, they come
to introduce themselves and tell me how afraid they
were of me, but always add that they remember me as a
good teacher. Of all the compliments I received from my
erstwhile students, I cherish the one received from a person
who is now one of the top-most bureaucrats of the state. He
said, 'Madam, because of the sound foundation you gave us
in school, we have been able to achieve so much in life!'
I taught them English from the beginners up to the sixth
class besides helping out with physical exercise classes and
organizing school functions. Teaching entails a lot of hard
work and commitment but compliments like these are the
rewards that all teachers cherish.

The Struggle Within

On the surface, it appeared that my life was running on an
even keel as a teacher and as the wife of an MLA. Seeing my
public persona, no one could guess that there was always a
nagging uneasiness deep in my mind when I thought about
the future, especially of the children. The more I read about
the happenings in the world, the more I began to look at our
situation as stifling, limited and uninspiring. There seemed
to be a growing discontent in my mind about the quality of
life that we were leading; meeting the same set of people at
public functions and parties in the Deputy Commissioner's
home or Army Headquarters, going to church alone,
trudging to school every day, fine weather or foul. It was the
sameness of it all that seemed to drag me down. I needed
something more than what my present circumstances could
provide. But what? And then the all-important question: was
I competent or qualified enough to try to change it? It was

then that the long-dormant hankering after further studies once again surfaced and I began to think that since that was the only avenue open for me, I must try and obtain a university degree to look for a better job. But I suppose much more than that I needed to prove that I could do it in spite of the many difficulties that lay before me now. I had a full-time job, four children and a politician husband. Where would I get the time to study even if the local college, by now known as Fazl Ali College with a regular Principal and lecturers, gave me permission to appear as a non-collegiate student from their college? But the compulsions from within were inexorable; I decided to seek permission from the college to write the B.A exam and an understanding Principal gladly gave me the required permission.

In those days, I am referring to the seventies, Gauhati University had the system of two-part exams for the B.A. and B.Sc. degrees. So I began studying for the B.A Part I exam in right earnest. Every one, including myself sometimes, thought that I was crazy and too ambitious in attempting to take on what seemed to be an impossible task given my circumstances. I had a big family to look after, my husband was a politician and besides, I was a full-time teacher in a school. But the die was cast and I was determined to go ahead with my plan. In order to achieve this audacious goal, I had to put a firm routine in place to cram study hours into the already hectic schedule I was following. The only way was to get up earlier than usual. So I put the alarm at 2 am every morning so that I would get some quiet and free time to study before the children woke up, which was usually at about 5 am. This way I could snatch about three hours of study every day. Looking back, I can say that those were the most taxing days of my life when my mental and physical strength was stretched to the extreme.

Those days we did not have gas stoves or any other mode

of cooking except firewood. So as soon as I got up, I would go to the kitchen, separated from the main house by a corridor, light the fire, make myself a huge cup of tea and settle down to serious study. As it happens, for me the morning hours are the best part of the day and anything I read during this period is better retained, even now. Of course on some mornings a child would wake up early clamouring for mother and I had to hold her on my lap as I tried to concentrate on the book. By the time the children woke up, the books had to be stowed away until the next morning. And the preparations for going to school would begin in right earnest, setting aside all thoughts of books and exams. This was the routine that I followed for both Part I and Part II B.A exam the next year.

The results were declared at the end of the Part II exams, and to my great surprise, and I suppose to most people's, I passed with Distinction, securing the 3rd position in the University. When the mark sheets were received in the college, the Principal, (Late) Prof. Asraf Ali came to our school to congratulate me and to encourage me to go for a M.A. in English as I had secured excellent marks in the subject. His words were like the trigger that signalled the beginning of another phase in my life. I took his words seriously and began to ask myself whether I was capable of pursuing this goal, given my circumstances. My husband was still in politics and he was away from the house frequently on account of Assembly meetings and also in connection with his business concerns. Then one Sunday, another important person of the town (late) Mr. Mayangnokcha came to visit my father-in-law. He was the retired Head Master of the Government High School and was held in great esteem by the townspeople because during his career he had spurned a Government offer of an administrative job in order to continue teaching. He was earlier decorated with the OBE by the erstwhile British rulers.

After they chatted for a while, he sent for me ostensibly to congratulate me on my success. He made me sit beside him and in the presence of my father-in-law urged me to do a M.A. in English and said that he had been closely monitoring my scholastic pursuits over the years and believed that I was capable of greater things. Turning to my father-in-law he said that he should be proud of such a daughter-in-law. My father-in-law did not say anything, just nodded his head. I sometimes wonder about this visit and ask myself whether the wise old man had heard about the initial opposition of the family to my pursuit of higher studies and was now actively trying to help me find a way to this goal. But regardless, I remain grateful to him for this encouraging gesture.

Having received encouragement from two important personages of the town, I began to think seriously about going to university. When I attempted the B.A. exams, I was solely motivated by the prospect of receiving a higher scale of pay! But now I could dream of teaching in a college if I succeeded in obtaining an M.A. degree. It was all heady stuff for a mere housewife trying to cope with four children and a demanding job at school. And of course there was my husband; what would he say to this pipe dream of mine? He was away from home when the visits happened and when he came home, I timidly told him what they said, especially that bit about father-in-law being present during the second visit. I also declared that if I did the M.A. course it would have to be as a regular student, not as a private candidate for which the University had provisions. The private M.A. degrees did not have much value as far as job prospects were concerned, I added. He kept quiet for a long time; and to my great delight he told me that if that was what I really wanted, he would not stand in the way. He even said that he would personally escort me to Gauhati to seek admission in the course as the last date for submission of applications was about to expire.

This is how I had my first plane ride from Jorhat to Gauhati in an old Dakota(I think)! It seemed so amazing that we reached our destination before I could take in the excitement of this novel plane ride. After some initial hurdles faced because of my late application, the admission process was done and we came back in a bus from Gauhati to Jorhat and then in our jeep to our home in the hills. Though I did feel excited about becoming a 'student' once more at this stage in my life, there were many doubts in my mind about leaving the children to the care of servants and foisting this additional burden on my husband. There were also protests from relatives in the village; they thought I was becoming too ambitious and reneging on my duties as a mother and wife. My youngest paternal uncle came up from the village to find out if this project indeed had my husband's approval. I understood their concern because I too was becoming apprehensive as the day of my departure to Gauhati approached. I shed secret tears at night but could not back out now, all the time trying to convince myself that I was doing this for the good of the family.

I would be failing in my moral duty if I do not mention the devoted service of a person called Bir Bahadur Gurung who had come to us as a bodyguard of my husband after he was elected the first time. He was a simple man, spoke mostly in his mother tongue Nepali and before we realized it, took over the running of the household. The children were at first wary of him but with the intuitive wisdom of the innocent they recognized the inherent goodness and generosity of his heart and he soon won them over. Once the initial reserve between them was overcome, he became their best friend and mentor. And by and by he even seemed to have usurped our position with the children because when something happened to them, unlike the earlier screams for 'mommy' or 'daddy', it became 'Gurung'! Gradually but unobtrusively Gurung became an integral part of our family and I too began to rely on him for the management of the house more and more as days went by. And incidentally, his being there with the children when I was going to be away at university considerably relieved my mind, though the nagging guilt persisted. Gurung remained with us till a year after we moved to Shillong in 1975. He went to Nepal saying that he would come back but the last time I saw him was that day when I bid farewell to this gem of a person at the bus stop, a man who had virtually adopted our family and looked after us so devotedly for nearly twelve years. I must also add that to a very great extent his presence at home facilitated my university venture. I could not express my gratitude properly that day because I expected to see him again; so what I am trying to articulate here is my indebtedness to a simple soul from another country and another clime who taught me the true meaning of devotion: that as long as you had love in your heart everyone is your family, everyone is your friend. We missed him and hoped that he would appear at our doorstep one day, but that day never came. I only hope that he had a good life wherever he went. Jai ho Gurung!

It so happened that my roommate in the university hostel was also married and had a young son. Her husband was a Doctor who had encouraged her to come to university because she was a brilliant student of Philosophy. When one of us was overwhelmed by homesickness and guilt at leaving our family behind, the other would try to cheer her up by saying that it was only for two years, not forever. But right then two years indeed sounded forever but we soon learnt that if we fulfilled the minimum requirement of attendance, we could write our exams as regular students. This is how I stayed the minimum required days in the hostel and made frequent trips home to be with my children and husband. Before leaving for the university, I had resigned from my job in the school for the last time and during my stay at home during these periods I could not only study freely but also take care of the children. We did two exams, M.A. Part I and II during these two years and before we knew it, the course was over! Both my room-mate and I did well and in my resume, I could proudly write M.A. English. Incidentally, I secured the 2nd position in the university.

When I look back on this particular aspect of my life, I realize how much the approval and support of my husband contributed to the eventual success in my endeavours. Deep in my heart I have always felt grateful to him for understanding my urges and I regret that I may not have expressed this to him when we were together. But I remember an incident when my eldest brother told him how much my family appreciated his role in my success. He had not finished college, giving up academic pursuit after the Intermediate Science exams. But being a practical man, he must have recognized the ultimate good that my efforts would bring to the children and their future. The profession that he was more or less forced to accept could never be relied upon to provide a sound foundation to them. Nor would the government contracts which were now being monopolized by craftier and wealthier people come his way as before because he was an MLA now. Whatever reserves we had were more or less spent on three election campaigns and our income had to be supplemented by my efforts. Besides this, I have a lurking feeling that he believed that my academic career was halted when I had to get married to him and this awareness may have persuaded him to support my attempts at higher studies.

Our last election was held in 1974 after I obtained my M.A. degree. It was a disaster and we lost badly. One would have thought that it was the end of my husband's political career but his party colleagues would not let him go so easily and he remained a politician till the end. This fiasco saw us move out of Mokokchung to Kohima where I got a job in the Arts College there as a Lecturer. But I did not stay there long as I was selected as a Lecturer in the North-Eastern Hill University in 1975 where I served till October 2010. Before this appointment however, I had to cross another hurdle. During a trip to Shillong to put our son in St. Edmund's Boarding school, I visited the office of the North-Eastern Hill University and submitted an application for the post of Lecturer, enclosing all my certificates and mark-sheets starting from Matriculation exam. I assumed that a newly-set up university would surely need teachers and thought that I had a fair chance because of my good academic records. I soon forgot about it. But when the then Vice-Chancellor of the University, (Late) Dr. C. Devanesan came to visit the Kohima Campus of the University, he came to meet me and gave me a few suggestions which eventually helped me to get a job in the University. He said that applications like the one I submitted cannot be considered just like that. It had to be in response to an advertisement of the University, which they had not yet done. Secondly he said that I would need an all-important Diploma which was an essential qualification for the post of a Lecturer in English in NEHU then: Diploma in the Teaching of English. I suppose it was the equivalent of the NET qualification these days which is a must for all aspirants at the entry level. He added that if I wanted to acquire this Diploma, he could arrange a seat for me in the Central Institute of English and Foreign Languages at Hyderabad where the Director was known to him. Without a moment's hesitation I accepted his offer.

It was only when he and his officers left, that I realized that it was the first spontaneous decision I had taken for any course of action all on my own without consulting my husband first and acquiring his approval. This did not go down well with him; but then he also did not openly oppose it. As for me it was a momentous decision because it meant that I would be away from home and the children for two semesters, which is a year. It would not be like paying flying visits to Gauhati during my M.A. days because the Institute, I learnt, was very strict on attendance, deducting from the stipend even for a day's absence without proper leave. The stint in CIEFL was one of the most difficult periods of my life because of the increasing estrangement from my husband on the one hand and the necessity to cope with the tough subjects in the very limited time span on the other. I do not remember ever going to bed before 1am during the two semesters I was there because on top of attending classes from 9 in the morning till 5 in the afternoon with only an hour's break for lunch, we were required to write assignments everyday for submission the following morning. The credits went into our internal assessment. Having taken the momentous decision to enrol in the Institute, I did not want give up easily and after coping with the gruelling routine, eventually I came home with a decent Diploma!

The way I look at it now, my unilateral decision to do the Diploma course was my first act of independence, may be even of defiance. My husband must have sensed that in a certain way I was moving away from the ambit of his control and coming into my own. If I had taken a job in a college within the state, he certainly would not have felt slighted or threatened in any way. But the inevitable was happening and when the advertisement from NEHU appeared in newspapers, I applied, was interviewed in Delhi and was selected. I considered it as a personal achievement but everyone else in our families expressed doubts about the wisdom of accepting the offer which would certainly result in bringing about the physical- dislocation of the family. But as far as I was concerned, this was the crucial change of fortune that I had hankered after through my academic pursuits. It would give me a certain status, and through this all the children would be able to study in the best schools in Shillong where the university was located. I was clear in my mind; there could be no turning back now from such a prospect, I would not deny myself and the children this opportunity, no matter what the cost.

As apprehended, our move to Shillong was indeed the beginning of the disintegration of our family as a cohesive unit. My husband could not or would not come to Shillong on a permanent basis on account of his politics and business; he came only for short visits. Other elements intruded on the husband-wife equation and the emotional distance widened as the years went by. We both became victims of our own egos and personal indiscretions. The marriage was on the brink of collapse and the only recourse then was to have a clean break, which happened in 1978. After we moved to Shillong in 1975 the daughters were enrolled in Loreto Convent and the son continued at St. Edmund's School as a day scholar where he was earlier a boarder. They remained with me all through their school and college years though they regularly spent holidays with their father.

At this point I want to elaborate on a remarkable custom among us which gives a lot of psychological support to children of broken marriages. There are usually no bitter custody fights over them, nor is there any harmful stigma attached to their being such children. They are made welcome in both their father's and mother's families; their status never changes on account of their parents' being divorced. Even when the father married again, the children's rights as the first-borns were never in dispute in his household. So was the case with the paternal uncles and aunts. It seemed that there was no change for them except the fact that their father and mother did not live together anymore. Whatever acrimony there was earlier ended when the divorce became final. For me too, I may have ceased to be their daughter-in-law, but I continued to be the mother of their grandchildren and the respect due to this status was never denied to me. In fact, I often visited my in-laws whenever I found myself in places where they lived. I had very close relationship with my eldest sister-in-law which we maintained until her death some years ago. This was possible because the system had been in place ever since our village societies were established. What the families were doing was actually to ensure that the children, who belonged to their clans, did not suffer, not only physically but mentally also just because two individuals decided that they could not live with one another any more. By extending their emotional support, and often economic assistance too, they were nurturing the next generation. From my own experience I can say that such social support system shows a lot of maturity and a highly evolved sense of civilized behaviour.

When my husband died in 1993, I was serving in Dimapur and went with the children to attend his funeral at Kohima. If I had not gone, it would have been construed as a dereliction of expected behaviour unless of course if I was bed-ridden or out of the country. One of my nieces was surely intrigued because there was the second wife as the chief mourner and my presence there must have seemed so out of place. She could not contain her curiosity and almost apologetically asked, "Aunty, are you still in love with uncle?" I was taken aback by the directness of her question but understood her confusion. I paused a while before I replied. "I don't know whether you can still call it love; but I have borne this man five children and I had to be here today to bid him farewell." It is indeed difficult to say what it was that I felt for this man at that moment: love or merely a sense of duty and obligation as the father of my children? Or was it even guilt that I had left him behind in my pursuit for a better future? What I could not articulate then is about the hallowed circle of life which we had inhabited for a greater part of the last 34 years and brought 5 children into the world. It was now broken with his death though the legality of that bond had been annulled 15 years earlier. But the physical connectedness had decidedly created a brand of loyalty on account of which I had come to pay my last respects to the father of my children. Our tragedy was that we could not end our days within that circle because this loyalty could not be sustained as it was not bolstered by stronger emotional ties. But all the same, there I was, trying to give a logical explanation to a young girl who still saw life in black and white.

Perhaps I will never be able to give a definite answer to the question posed by my niece. But on that day during the funeral service, when my son spoke on behalf of the children, I cried when I recognized the deep anguish in his heart at the loss of his father even as he manfully held himself back from breaking down in public. But I shed silent tears in commiseration with their sorrow, as also from a self-indictment: that even when he was alive, the children were deprived' of a father's presence and guidance during the formative years of their lives. I only hope that my children will forgive me some day for being the instrument of this deprivation.

University Life

After the initial euphoria of becoming a University Lecturer, I found out to my great distress what it entailed. I dreaded entering the classroom where the students sat with a variety of expressions. The brighter ones with open cynicism, the others with bland unseeing eyes examining the newest teacher's physical appearance and sometimes sniggering when they thought I was looking elsewhere. The teaching assignment was also stupendous; all the texts that were rejected by the others became my lot to tackle, novels like *Middlemarch, Dombey and Sons, Point Counterpoint, Portrait of a Lady* etc. What I did in M.A. was a kind of selective reading after consulting the previous year's question papers and most of the NEHU M.A. texts were not on the Gauhati University syllabus, which meant that I had to read them first myself before I could discuss them in an intelligent way in the class. The first year was truly an ordeal and seeing me read so much, one of my daughters declared, "If this is what teachers have to do, I'll never become a teacher!" But I think I did not fare too badly either. On the other hand, the Language papers were a breeze because they were still fresh in my mind from my CIEFL classes and I had all my assignment papers with me to help in preparing the lectures. After the initial misgivings I discovered how much I enjoyed teaching these young adults who were always alert in class and participated in the discussions. Some of the students from the batch I taught that first year went on to become teachers in colleges and some even became my colleagues in the University later.

In the meantime, I was also trying to cope with a family of four school-going children as a single parent and at the same time looking after household chores. Life was made somewhat easy when there was a servant around but after our old servant went off to Nepal I had to depend on local dailies, who were not regular in attendance and selective in what they did around the house. To complicate matters, there was the question of income. In the seventies, a Lecturer's pay was not even a fraction of what it is today. The compulsory payments were the children's school fees, the cost of maintaining their uniforms and various other collections demanded by the schools, the house rent and most important of all food for a family of five. It was indeed a trying time and so when the University offered me the job of a Hostel Warden, I gladly accepted the offer because it would mean saving on house rent as I was given a house. So we moved in to our new home after staying in rented houses for three years. The job of a Warden in a hostel with more than sixty girls was demanding but I persevered and discharged my duties diligently for six and half years.

I was soon reminded by the senior teachers that I had to obtain a Ph.D. degree if I ever wanted to move up the scale, otherwise I would retire as a Lecturer only. So I began to think seriously about it and registered for it under the Supervisorship of the then Head of the Department, Dr. D.P. Singh. It was tough going, this research business. During the day and till about 9 in the evening my time would be occupied by teaching, supervising the children's needs and looking after the hostel administration. So my reading and writing for this project would begin only after 10 in the evening. Since I was highly motivated to finish this task soon, I used to sit till 1 am and sometimes even beyond to finish a particular section of my writings. In those days, one wrote by hand and if you wanted to change something in a paragraph, you had to write the whole thing over again; very tedious and time-consuming but there were no computers then at least in our environment. When I think back on those days, I truly appreciate the liberating and time-saving facilities that gadgets like computers today have brought to students and writers alike. Anyway, slog I did and submitted my thesis to the University and was awarded the degree in 1983. That same year I applied for and was selected as a Reader in the Department of English, NEHU.

Minnesota Memories

I had always been fascinated by our folktales and had begun
to take a keen interest in my own folklore. I had started to
collect folktales with the intention of translating them into
English and publish a book. For this I got a small grant for
a minor project from the UGC. During this period, I came
across an advertisement calling for candidates to apply for
the Fulbright Fellowships. Seeing that Culture Studies was
one of the subjects, I applied and to my great surprise I
was awarded a Fulbright Fellowship to go to the University
of Minnesota in the USA where I would be attached to the
American Indian Studies Department. The time span from
3 months to a year was left to the discretion of the selected
candidate. So I chose a period when the children would have
their holidays and decided to stay abroad for only 3 months.
On the appointed day I boarded an Air India Maharaja flight
from Delhi and embarked on this trip without the slightest clue
as to what one should do in order to reach one's destination
safely. The one phone call I made from the airport was to
the Head of the Department there requesting him to receive
me at the airport at Minneapolis. But my itinerary showed
that there was to be a halt at New York for one night and
like the fool that I was, I had no contingency plan for this.
I simply thought that I would request the airlines people to
arrange a cheap hotel for me for the night and embark on
the last leg for Minnesota the next morning. I did not realize
the enormity of the risk I was taking until I got to talking
with an Indian lady travelling to New York solely to keep her
Green Card up to date and valid.

From Delhi up to London via a stop at Dubai, the plane
was half empty and I had noticed a lady lying down on all
three seats in her row. When we got down in London airport
we visited the Duty Free shop and it was while trying to board

the plane again that I realized that my passport and tickets were not with me! While the other passengers were allowed in, a few of us were detained in a corner while the airlines personnel tried to locate our documents in the various seats we had occupied. I was panic-stricken imagining all kinds of worst-case scenarios when I noticed that a huge man was grinning at me. He came nearer and said, "Madam, don't worry, we'll spend the night together in London!" Seeing my shocked expression he burst out laughing and said, "Don't worry, everything will be fine." It seems he was a Pakistani and a seasoned traveller but he had left his papers in the pocket of his jacket on his seat while dis-embarking. And sure enough, the Air India Liaison Officer brought me my ticket and passport and with a huge sigh of relief I boarded the plane for the onward journey to New York, along with the Pakistani gentleman.

It was during this part of the journey that I got to talking with the Indian lady who was at first surprised when I told her that I was Indian too. She then asked where I was going and when I told her about it the first question she asked me was where I was going to stay the night in New York. I replied, 'I don't know' and then told her about my plan of asking the airlines people to help me find a room. She was shocked beyond words, she simply looked at me for a long while wondering perhaps what kind of an idiot I was, taking things so lightly. She then said, "You are mad, this is New York my dear and you cannot trust anyone around here." She seemed to have come to a decision; turning to me she said, "You are coming with me and I will see to it that you get on that plane tomorrow morning to Minneapolis." So she took me to her apartment which was very close to the United Nations building, which is the only landmark I remember now and from her apartment on the 18th floor I could also see the Empire State Building. We went out to a nearby store to buy some provisions and I spent a safe and restful night because of the generosity and concern of this kind lady. Her name was Raj, she said and most of the time she lived in Delhi, coming to the States only to renew her Green Card. She seemed to be very rich; her eldest son was a businessman currently in France. She showed me his wardrobe which was crammed full of his clothes and things and she also told me that they had apartments in Paris and London too. In all these places too, they kept everything they would need and they travelled with only a small briefcase! But there was a recent tragedy in their family; their younger son who was studying at Berkley met with an accident in the car which was presented to him by the parents for his birthday just a few months earlier. She was still mourning him and I saw on the plane that she was constantly touching her prayer beads even as she was talking to me. This particular gesture of kindness from a total stranger confirms my faith in the goodness of the human heart. I hope she's had a good life and sometimes I regret that that I did not keep in touch with her.

There was another incident on the plane when I met two attendants who were eagerly waiting to talk to me. They were told that someone from North-East India was on board and they were very excited. The young girl said she was from Assam and the boy, a little senior to her was from Manipur. They couldn't spend too much time with me as they were on duty but the young steward managed to give me a gift hamper which contained a bottle of red wine, some maps and things like that and a pair of warm house socks. I was really touched and realized how homesick they too were and what it must have meant for them to meet and talk to someone of their own kind in a plane flying miles above the earth. Talk of nostalgia for one's homeland! However they were not the only ones who missed their homeland; after the excitement and euphoria of landing myself in a 'foreign' land, that too, America waned, I too began to feel terribly lonely and miserable in the strange environment. The fact that I went there in October and the snow started falling soon after, did not help matters at all. The swirling snowflakes soon draped trees, housetops and parked cars. The ground became stark white and slippery and I began having nightmares: what if I fell and broke a limb? Though I helped my landlady, Judy, to put insulating putty on windows and tiny cracks in the house, the outside world looked bleak and forbidding. The distance from home also felt further and I refused to look at any map while I was there so that I could blank out this vast physical barrier between America and the tiny dot that was Shillong on these maps. Sometimes I even had this weird notion: when I eventually went back, would I still find Shillong and my home in the same place? What if that little speck on the earth had disappeared when I was away? So when the plane touched down at Delhi airport on my return, I was almost in tears and felt like kneeling down and kissing the ground in thanksgiving for coming back home in one piece!

But in spite of this well-concealed anxiety about being so far away from home, my stay in Minnesota was one of the most memorable periods of my life. While still in India, I had agreed to stay as a paying guest in the home of Ron and Judy Libertus for the duration of my stay there. Ron had sent a student to pick me up from the airport, a boy called Malcolm. When we reached the office, I gave him the bottle of wine by way of thanks and he was thrilled. Ron took me around the Department and introduced me to all the people I would be seeing for the next three months and then he took me home. Judy was eagerly waiting for us and showed me my room and bathroom and said that I could use their kitchen to cook my food. From that very first day

I felt at home with these warm-hearted people and knew that I would not have to worry about anything. Later when we became more relaxed with each other, Judy told me how shocked she was to meet me for the first time! When I asked her why she said, "Look, they said that an Indian woman was coming to stay with us and I was expecting someone with a dark complexion, wearing a sari, long braided hair, with a red blob on the forehead and with a smattering of English. But there you were, fair, with bobbed hair, wearing jeans and speaking better English than me, wouldn't I be shocked?" and then she giggled. My appearance made many people believe that I was not Indian-Indian and some wits went to the extent of saying that Ron, who himself had Native American blood, was playing a practical joke on his friends by trying to fob off one of his cousins from the Reservation as an Indian-Indian!

Perhaps it was because of the physical similarities that I found ready acceptance among the Native Americans who invited me to their dances, sweat lodge ceremonies and fry bread parties. I was attached to the Department devoted to the study of their Culture and History and by mingling with them and monitoring their Language and History classes I took away with me many precious lessons about the values of preserving one's own culture. On the other hand, Ron, the Professor and my landlord was considered to be a Native American because he had one-eighth of Native Indian blood, although he did not at all look like one. Anyone meeting him for the first time would think he was a white American but because of his remote blood tie, he was enumerated as a Native American. This itself gives us an indication about the demographic situation of the native tribes.

The Language classes were also a revelation; post-graduate students were being taught absolutely basic language skills by persons who had not even graduated from

High School. But they had to be employed as university teachers because they were among the few survivors who knew the native language, Ojibway in this case. I was told that this was the situation in Language classes for other tribes too. The History classes I monitored were all about the various battles the tribes fought with the British first and then with white Americans. Not only that, the lessons also included the innumerable litigations in US Courts that the Native Americans were still fighting to regain their land and water rights. I found the situation quite depressing because once you lose your language you lose your culture. And being deprived of their natural rights to original habitats and being herded into Reservations amounted to complete emasculation of the brave tribes, reducing them to a state of extreme dependency. Many young men and women turned to alcohol, drugs and crime. The few Native American sections of the city that I saw were poor, unkempt and dirty. The decadence was reflected in the physical features of the people too: most of them looked depressed and obese in a strangely misshapen way. During Thanksgiving that year, the Libertus family volunteered their services in the Community Hall of a church where free lunch was going to be provided to the poor and destitute of the city. I also accompanied them. And what I saw amazed me, because one could never imagine that amidst the prosperity and glamour of America, so much poverty and misery existed. When the counter opened, the line of dirty, dishevelled and some handicapped people began to be served a sumptuous lunch of roast turkey, cranberry sauce and other goodies. The remarkable thing was that among the mostly Black and Native American men and women in the lines waiting to be served, there were quite a few white Americans too. The lunch was sponsored by a rich industrialist of the city. The event was quite an eye-opener for me.

On the academic front I made good use of my time, short though it was and came back with quite a sizeable quantity of research material and references. There was an excellent library in the University and I spent much of my time there to collect these materials and catching up on reading books on folklore and cultures of other countries too. From the insights gained during my stay there I could put a broader perspective on my project and eventually it was expanded from only folktales to become the book, *The Ao-Naga Oral Tradition*.

On the whole I can say that my Minnesota experience widened my understanding of other people and other cultures and also made me aware how fortunate those of us are who can still speak their native languages and have not been totally dislodged from their roots. One weekend I accompanied Ron to a camp where young Native Americans were going to be taught how to build a tepee. I was in for a shock; the group went to a field where young pine trees were standing in rows, obviously a man-made plantation. They began using electric saws to cut down the required number of trees and the instructor began to demonstrate how to wrap the 'skins' (tarpaulins in this case) and plant the posts on the ground to look like a tepee. I could see that even the so-called instructor was inept at the job and the group took a long time to make the structure stand up like a tepee! I came away with some uneasy thoughts about the need to re-look at the way we try to 'preserve' or 're-visit' our old material cultures without the aid of any historical context of the people.

My mentors, Dr. and Mrs Hasselblad somehow came to know that I was in Minnesota. They called me and invited me to visit them in their home in Redlands, California. Dr. Hasselblad had retired from missionary service and they were now living in a retirement village or senior neighbourhood called Plymouth where every conceivable amenity was provided for. It was a self-contained enclave; they had their own little church, market and of course a central medical facility which was connected to every home there. In the one-story houses there were un-obtrusive bell-cords and buttons which could summon aid within seconds. I flew from Minneapolis to California where the good doctor and his wife received me at the airport. The next day they took me to the Joshua Tree National Park where a vast region was covered with just this one species of vegetation called the Joshua tree in all conceivable shapes and sizes. The park is said to cover an area of 790,636 acres with all the usual tourist facilities located at strategic points.

Driving to the park through the grand landscape around me was in itself a thrilling experience. For the first time after landing in America and being confined to snow-bound Minnesota, I was seeing the grandeur of the surrounding mountains, the wide expanses of land and was simply awestruck by the sheer vastness of it all and oh! the varied and vivid colours of the skies and the entire landscape! At some silly moment I even thought, how could God make all this? As if she guessed my thoughts, Mrs. Hasselblad told me casually that the police can patrol these vast regions only from helicopters. On my flight from Minneapolis, just before the short stop-over at Denver I remember the pilot directing us to view the Grand Canyons from the plane because it was at that point of time when the sun was dipping towards the west. What a spectacle it was! I still do not have the words to describe my emotions when with each passing moment the canyons changed colour with the angle of the sun over them. Recalling this, all through the drive that day, I was struck with the thought that perhaps because of the beautiful, grand and spectacular environment in which they live, the Americans can talk big, live big and give big!

While still in California, I had another chance to visit a famous landmark in America: Disneyland! It came about like this; when Ron Junior, who was working in California heard that I was there, he offered to take me to Disneyland because he was living in a nearby town from where I was. On the appointed day he came with his Vietnamese girl friend, Mei, to pick me up and away we went. I could not believe my luck. Disneyland was more than I could ever imagine; there were so many things one wanted to see and do. But we did not have enough time, so we chose a few things among the 'must do' items. We bought tickets for the roller-coaster ride through tunnels and underground passageways (I forget what it was called). For the 7 minute ride we had to stand in queue for 45 minutes! It was that popular. The speed of the passage and strange lights illuminating stranger animals lurking in the deep caverns who looked as if they were about to devour you made it the most frighteningly exhilarating ride. We also sailed down the Mississippi a la Huck Finn and company with real-looking animals on the banks watching our slow progress down the river. We went on the canoes that follow a meandering route where children from all over the world serenade you from the cliffs above the stream. And then there was this room where you feel the universe is advancing to engulf you! I forgot what it was called; after all it happened 26 years ago! I also stood behind huge cardboard cut-outs while they took photographs of me riding a horse or standing beside famous Americans! All in all I had a marvellous time in this fantastic man-made park designed to bring in a bit of magic and fantasy into ordinary lives. Even here, one could feel the American penchant for the big, the bold and the fantastic. As we drove back to Redlands, I wondered how many days or months one needed to see and do everything that Disneyland had to offer!

New Home

Living in rented houses and then the Warden's quarter rekindled my desire to have a home of my own. I thought that it would remove an apparent vulnerability from our family set-up. On a few occasions during their holidays, I had brought the children back to Nagaland but had to stay in my brother's home because I had no place in my old one. The children went and stayed with their father while I waited in my brother's place till the holidays were over and we could come back to Shillong together. I decided that the most practical thing would be to own a house in Shillong. After much effort and an agonizing wait, I managed to get a housing loan from the university and bought a small house. It was to this house that we moved after my return from the States. For me it marked another milepost in my struggle to keep the family together by providing a base for the children to grow up in and the nest to which they could return. Finally, I felt, there was a sense of cohesion and permanence in a family which was still a broken one in the eyes of outsiders. Perhaps my traditional background also had a role to play in my intense desire to live in my own home. I never felt at ease in rented houses, nor in the warden's quarter. Living in some one else's house was the equivalent of being 'homeless' in the traditional sense and all my conscious life I had fought against this status. So the acquisition of a house of my own was very important for us as a family and especially for my mental well-being.

Administrative Experience

In 1989, the post of a Professor in the Department fell vacant; I applied for it and was selected. Thus on the professional front also I was making steady progress. In the meantime the children too were doing well. In that year, one daughter got married, the other two graduated from college and my son, after completing his B.A. had gone on to Delhi to pursue his post-graduate studies. Then an unexpected opportunity presented itself: in 1992, the post of Director, North East Zone Cultural Centre in Dimapur was advertised and on the urging of family and well-wishers, I applied for the job. After due process of interview etc. I was selected. After obtaining Deputation leave from the university I joined the post on 1st September the same year.

One of the compelling reasons of opting for this job was the desire to complete the construction of a house in Dimapur. Soon after becoming a Professor I had begun to contemplate my future and the prospect of retirement. The question was, where would I like to settle eventually? If one went by only the advantages and disadvantages of Shillong and Dimapur, the former would definitely win hands down. But was I looking only for creature comforts or something more than that? And I told myself that I needed to be with my people; my brothers were settled in Dimapur, besides many nephews and nieces. Our village was at a reasonable distance and I could visit other relatives in times of need or celebrations and I would be able to speak my language most of the time. So with the help of my eldest brother I had acquired a small plot of land and with loans from all available sources including my General Provident Fund, I had started the construction some years earlier. It was in a moribund state because I could not supervise the work from Shillong.

Apart from this very selfish consideration, the activities of NEZCC interested me immensely because it dealt with everything cultural and the added bonus was that its purview was the entire North-East region. So when I was given the opportunity, I grabbed it with both hands and plunged into the activities with great enthusiasm. It was a whole new experience for me though it took me some time to grasp the art of moving files and writing notes etc. But the best part was that I had the opportunity to visit all the various states during the different folk festivals that we organized all throughout the year according to a plan which was formulated for every financial year. The officers and staff of the Centre, wary and watchful at first, became relaxed and very co-operative once they discovered that I was not a bureaucrat and did not stand on ceremony.

The other side of administering this office was the need to interact with the Governor of Nagaland who was the Chairman of the Governing Body. The Memorandum of Association of the Centre contains this stipulation because the NEZCC is located in Nagaland. During my tenure of five years I had the good fortune of working with four Governors, all of whom were very understanding and did not interfere with the normal functioning of the Centre. On the other hand, it was the bureaucrats from Delhi who constantly took an obstructionist view of our activities. The meetings with them, which were quite frequent, were frustrating most of the time and I seemed to be in their bad book because I was not an I.A.S officer like all the rest of the Directors in the six other Zonal Centres. Such encounters were an eye-opener for me when I came into direct contact with the supercilious and condescending attitude of the officers in the Department of Culture at the Centre. More often than not, folk artistes from our region too were not treated at par with those from other Centres. Why it was so, I could never understand. But in spite of such handicaps, we tried our best to continue with our efforts and proved that we were in no way inferior to the other regions in terms of talent or cultural richness. The co-operation extended by the other Directors was very heartening and the cultural exchange programmes, through

which we se sent our performers to their zones and theirs
came to us proved to be very successful.

The Shangyu Saga

If I were to name one significant accomplishment during my
tenure as Director of NEZCC, it would be the construction
of the Heritage Museum at Shangyu village in Mon district
of Nagaland which now houses a unique wood carving,
measuring 20'x 12' and 6' ft in thickness displaying
intricately carved panels on both sides. This sculpture has
been authenticated and acknowledged as an antique. It is
a famous work of art which has caught the attention and
admiration of connoisseurs of art not only at home but
abroad too. It has featured in famous art journals all over the
world. It was earlier kept in the house of the Angh of Shangyu
right next to the central hearth exposed to the fumes and
soot and one could also see that there were distinct signs of
disrepair where children had touched and even tried to prise
loose the different figures on the huge panel. The Museum
which was eventually built by NEZCC was inaugurated by
the then Chairman and H.E. the Governor of Nagaland Shri
O.P. Sharma on 25th April 1997.

The idea to build the museum came to me when I saw
a picture of the sculpture in an international journal about
a photographic exhibition of unique art from all over the
world. I was awe-struck. It was indeed amazing to know that
such a genius had lived and worked among a people who
have always been projected as barbaric and uncivilized. I
wanted to see this famous artefact for myself but instinctively
decided that some more information about its origin and
status had to be gathered first. So for a preliminary survey
I sent the Museum Curator of our Centre to go to Mon and
consult the District Cultural Officer and if possible go with

him to meet the Angh of Shangyu in order to find out what he thought of this precious heritage languishing by his fireside. That first visit was a fiasco because the Angh refused to give them an audience saying that he did not trust government people because they were all liars, promising many things and doing nothing.

The Angh's reaction was frustrating, to say the least but all the same I became more determined than ever to do everything possible to preserve this priceless heritage of our people. So after a week or so I sent the Exhibition Officer and told him that he had to bring back as many photographs of the sculpture as possible so that we could think of a way to insure its preservation in a safe environment – I was already thinking in terms of a separate building to house it. Through the help of the DCO and the Pastor of the local church, our people could take photographs not only of the sculpture but also of other artefacts and some of the Angh himself. I was delighted because we seemed to be making some progress towards entering into a dialogue with the elusive and opinionated chief.

Since some contact had been established with the chief, I decided that it was time for me to pay him a visit. I was accompanied by the Joint Director, the Engineer and some other officers. We stayed overnight in the Mon Circuit House. And the next morning started for Shangyu village where an appointment with the Angh had been brokered by the DCO. Earlier we were told at Mon that it is customary for visitors to the Angh's house always to carry gifts for him; otherwise he would be offended. We were stumped; we did not carry any gift for the great man! Luckily for us some one suggested that we try to get some liquor from the Assam Rifles canteen at Mon, which would be welcome by the Angh because he liked his booze! They said that like most of his tribe, he also smoked opium. I said to myself, opium was the Angh's lookout; the few bottles of liquor that we managed to buy would have to do for a first gift.

At the appointed hour, we entered his house with some trepidation: what if, seeing me, a woman, he refused to talk to us? Would he accept the fact that a woman could be the Director, the boss over men? Inside, we found that some other villagers were already seated around the fireplace and dominating the entire room, there was the famous sculpture that I had travelled over abominable roads from Dimapur to see for myself. It was indeed unique and I felt that all the physical hardships paled before its mystical grandeur. We were offered low stools to sit and I noticed that there was only one chair in the room at a distance from us waiting for its occupant. The DCO sitting next to me whispered in English that in the Angh's presence, every one else had to sit at a lower level. He made us wait, this royal personage, and I was beginning to despair thinking that he had changed his mind. But after what seemed a long wait, the Angh shuffled out from the inner rooms wearing a fur coat and dressed in the regalia of his exalted position, royal tattoo on his face, the traditional Angh's hat and the blue beads around his knees proclaiming his royal blood. These beads could be worn only by persons of the royal families. Such was the position of the Anghs among the Konyak Nagas even in the nineties.

The Angh spoke first at length and an interpreter translated what he said. The Angh's grouse was that beginning from the then Governor of Assam, B.K. Nehru's time, dignitaries had come to look at his 'picture', saying many sweet things but never keeping their promises. He complained that waiting for them to repair his home he had lost a substantial portion of his royal abode. The interpreter told us that at one time, the house measured 60ft. lengthwise and about 24ft. breadth wise. The inside was divided by a corridor and there were separate rooms on both sides which housed the many concubines the Angh had at one time. Traditionally an Angh could take as many concubines as he wished. But only the children from his first wife, who had to be from another Angh clan, would be his legitimate children and the eldest son would succeed the father. All other children born to the Angh from his concubines were considered to be commoners like the other villagers. By the time we made contact with the Angh, he was past his prime and we were told by the DCO that at present, he had only a 'few' concubines, four or five, he said. The upkeep of the huge house was also becoming a problem, so the length was reduced to about half its size. The old man seemed to ramble at times about his ancestry, claiming that the ancestors of the Konyaks and Ahoms of Assam were brothers. He pointed to an ancient and huge gun reclining on a wall and said that it was a gift from the Ahom Raja to his ancestor. I noticed 4 or 5 elephant tusks also beside the gun and following my gaze the Angh said that someone had recently stolen a tusk from his house while he was sleeping. I thought to myself, 'More likely after a royal dose of opium!'

When I tried to steer the almost one-sided conversation to the sculpture in his house, the Angh began to talk about repairing his house instead, saying that it was why he had agreed to talk to us! I conferred with our people and told him frankly that our purpose was to build another house for the sculpture only. The Angh stood his ground at first; but when he saw that were equally adamant, he insisted that in that case then, we had to provide a similar hearth for him beside his 'picture'! My heart sank; I thought that my trip had been in vain. I knew that the old man understood Nagamese, the lingua-franca among Nagas, but he spoke only in his language while the interpreter spoke to us in Nagamese. Once or twice I caught the Angh reprimanding the interpreter for misinterpreting and he had to give us the right version of what his chief was saying. The meeting lasted for about an hour only but I was mentally exhausted and came away feeling defeated.

But I did not give up and planned to visit the Angh after a fortnight so that we could once again negotiate with him for a piece of land on which to build the museum to house the sculpture. Before the second trip, I instructed the office to buy a very good 'foreign' blanket from the local Hong Kong Market of Dimapur and included the engineer again among the delegation. The Angh was happy with the gift as it was winter and for the second audience he came out in an obviously ladies' overcoat with a fur collar! He began the meeting with his usual denouncement of Naga sahibs and named a few who, according to him 'ate' up the money that the government had given for repairing his house. I promptly answered by saying that we were not from the state government and that we had our orders from the Centre only and they would never allow us to repair an old house in Nagaland, Angh or no Angh. This made him sober up and he began to comprehend that we had a different agenda.

The Konyaks are a very intelligent and 'inventive' tribe among the Nagas. They are the only tribe who could make their own muzzle-loading guns and the gun powder for the weapons from simple indigenous ingredients. Historians claim that because they could not be handled as easily as the other tribes, the British introduced opium among them as a means of keeping them subdued for better administrative control. The Shangyu Angh also was addicted to the drug. So at times it became very difficult to reason with him and convince him that our sole concern was the protection and preservation of this priceless heritage. When we spoke about the sculpture, he would often refer to the mysterious circumstances under which it was made and brought to his village. In itself it is a fascinating legend but at that point of time our primary goal was to convince him to give us a plot of land where the 'museum', as I envisaged it, could be built.

During one of his ramblings, he happened to mention my eldest brother's name and said that he was good a friend of his. I remembered my brother had been the Deputy Commissioner of Mon for a number of years. At the mention of his name, I blurted out that he was my brother; the Angh looked sceptical at first but when the others of our group affirmed it, his whole demeanour seemed to change. He was no longer 'playing' with us and I sensed that this was a turning point in our dialogue and that he would give our proposal a serious consideration. And just as I hoped, he did. The next trip I made to Shangyu was to identify the plot of land for the museum and enter into an agreement with him that we would start construction immediately.

For funds for the project I had applied to the Department of Culture in the Human Resource Ministry, but the response was almost dismissive. So I took the matter up with the Finance Committee of NEZCC with a complete file on the project including a write-up on the legendary sculpture and also a blue print of the proposed building. The Committee gave its approval and the work started in right earnest. It was towards the end of 1996 and time was of the essence because my tenure was coming to an end in August the next year. It had become a project dear to my heart and I wanted to see it completed before I left the Zonal Centre.

The Shangyu Angh, whose name was Luhpong, was the chief Angh over thirteen other satellite villages in the area who paid him an annual tribute in the form of produce from a designated field in every village. So when the building was completed, all the thirteen lesser Anghs came to Shangyu for the installation of the sculpture in its new lodgings. Along with it, the Angh also allowed the gifts

from the Ahom Raja, the ivory tusks and many mithun and
buffalo skulls as well as some typical Konyak artefacts to
be housed in the building. For the inauguration of the new
building which I named Heritage Museum, I had invited
the Chairman of NEZCC, His Excellency the Governor of
Nagaland. He very graciously agreed to do so, travelling in
a helicopter from Kohima, thus avoiding the tortuous and
rough road to Shangyu.

It was an impressive occasion; we had brought folk
dancers from nearby villages as well as two Assamese troupes
from a border town. The Angh excelled himself on that day,
appearing in a tiger striped long coat of unidentifiable origin
and armed with his own gun. He wore a colourful hat and
had a pipe in his mouth. But the biggest shock for me was
when the local dancers accompanied their steps with loud
reports from their muzzle loaders! For a second I thought
that we were under attack from the underground forces and
I immediately looked at the Governor sitting next to me on
the bamboo dais constructed for the occasion. He seemed
unperturbed and I realized that though it was a first time
shocker for me, he must seen these dances so many times
before that he was used to the spectacle of dust, the loud
bangs and the acrid smell of gun powder obscuring the
frenzied dancers on the field.

When I made my final trip to Shangyu for the inauguration,
we bought a live pig for the Angh as a farewell gift. But the
crafty old man out-did us; without seeking our permission,
he had already ordered that a mithun be slaughtered to feed
the satellite Anghs under him who had assembled for the
inauguration as well as the sizeable local crowd. We were
simply told that the cost of the animal had to be borne by
us! Faced with the *fait-accompli*, the money was handed over
and later the Accounts section had to juggle their figures
because the Auditors would have taken a serious view of the

expenditure if the Account Head showed the amount as the 'cost of one mithun for Shangyu Angh'! It suddenly dawned on me that being in the state that he was, the Angh might demand some more money from us and to avoid such an eventuality, I decided to leave the celebrations soon after the Governor's departure. Before leaving, I instructed the Joint Director not to entertain any more demands from the Angh saying that only the Director could sanction any money and that she had been called away on an urgent matter.

There was no formal leave-taking from this very shrewd and intriguing Angh who represented a dying tradition of feudalism among the Konyak Nagas. Incidentally, he died a few years ago and his son whose name is L. Ame Angh inherited his father's throne. Through my interaction with the late Angh, I had the privilege of learning a lot of interesting things about this ancient institution among the Konyak Nagas whose power was slowly beginning to be eroded by the introduction of democratic systems like the village councils which devolved power to his erstwhile subjects. He gave us the land because, I am sure, that he too had sensed that his days were over and that a new order would soon replace the old. But as long as he lived, he tried to hold on to his heritage as best as he could and maintained proper decorum befitting his status. I felt a bit guilty as I drove away almost stealthily knowing that we had taken advantage of the Angh's vulnerability on account of his being poised on the brink of transition from the ancient to the modern. I am sure that his capitulation to our request in the end was helped along by the advice of council members with whom we'd had lengthy sessions about the developments which would surely follow if the sculpture was housed in a proper museum. We had earlier been told that the Angh's royal wife had converted to Christianity before her death; we also saw her grave in the compound. Therefore we enlisted the help of the Pastor and I am sure that he too encouraged the Angh to grant us our request. On account of these pressures the Angh must have realized how his absolute sway was waning right before his eyes; but then such is the inexorable tide of history that have levelled more powerful kings and emperors than the out-dated Angh of Shangyu living out his twilight years in a remote village among the hills and jungles of a slice of earth called Nagaland. I did not see it then; but now know that my role in that inevitable process has become more than an incidental detail in my resume.

I tried to convince myself that what we had accomplished was for all and that he too would share the credit for conceding that the sculpture would henceforth belong to all Nagas, though Shangyu would be its secure resting place and the Angh its permanent host. All in all, the Shangyu Saga ended on this self-congratulatory note and in the subsequent Governing Body Meeting of the Centre before I demitted office, my proposal for handing over the Museum to the Government of Nagaland was approved. It was done because NEZCC did not have any infra-structure outside Dimapur for the supervision and upkeep of the Museum. It was a smooth transfer of responsibility because such a move was already provided for in the Memorandum of Association of the Centre. I breathed easy knowing that the precious art specimen was now not only housed in a safer building but that the government agencies there would ensure its continued safety for posterity to marvel at the handiwork of the Naga genius who had chipped away (for how long?) in the deep jungle according to the legend, to carve this beauty out of one single piece of wood.

The other aspect of my tenure at NEZCC, though less tangible, is the rapport that the Centre was able to establish with artistes and officers of member-states within its ambit which ensured the success of festivals and strengthened the sense of belonging and brotherhood among the various communities.

My two year tenure as Director was renewed thrice and NEHU also extended my deputation period each time. But the 3rd renewal was halved because university Ordinances do not permit extension of deputation beyond five years. So after five years of hectic 'cultural' activities, I came back to my job in the university a little more knowledgeable about file-pushing and 'administrative' matters. But the greatest gain has been the cultural knowledge gleamed from the different ethnic groups of our fascinating region. Incidentally, I could also do some substantial construction of my house at Dimapur. But I want to add here that the life I led as Director of the centre is not something that I could have endured much longer. I was beginning to grow restless; the need to be on the move all the time and having to cope with opinionated babus in Delhi who had little regard for the North-East was unsettling my mental equilibrium. I had begun to miss classroom teaching and the sedate and calm existence of university life. So when I rejoined NEHU in September 1997, it was like a second homecoming for me. After my return, I became the Head of the Department of English for a tenure of three years and subsequently served as Dean, School of Humanities and Education of NEHU for two consecutive terms from 2004 to 2010.

Foreign Trips

During the last part of my tenure in NEHU, I got several opportunities to visit some foreign countries as a member of delegations from the Sahitya Akademi, New Delhi. The first trip was to China where we visited Beijing, Sichuan and Shanghai. When we were driven through the main city for our first meeting with Chinese intellectuals, the sheer 'modernity' of the city was so blatant and intense that a member of the delegation exclaimed, '*Arre, yeh to Manhattan ka bhi baap nikla!*' The most remarkable and memorable experiences included visits to the Forbidden City where we crossed doors after ornate doors to gape at the intricate architecture, the neat gardens and the innumerable artefacts inside rooms when could get a peep, intricate designs adorning doorways, porches and even rooftops. And then there was the walk through the (in)famous Tiananmen Square in comparative silence amidst the bustling crowds, left to our own inner emotions. We also ventured on to a section of the Great Wall where all of us attempted to climb as many steps as possible. Some in our group, the Secretary, Mr. A. Krishna Murthy included, reached a certain point in the climb for reaching which a plaque is given in recognition of their feat. When the men came down proudly displaying their prizes, most of us were sitting on the steps in exhaustion and eager to climb down!

The next marvellous experience was when we were taken to see the world famous terracotta figures in the pits of Xian in Shaanxi province. These pits, which were discovered in 1974 by some local farmers, are said to contain 8,000 life-size warriors, 130 chariots, 520 horses and 150 cavalry horses. They were installed there to protect the first Emperor of China, Qin Shi Huang in his afterlife, a scenario somewhat reminiscent of the elaborate tombs of the Pharaohs of Egypt. Some restoration work was also going on, where the experts showed us the extremely painstaking methods employed to restore the figures with all their features intact. We saw only a portion of the location of these warriors and their horses, but whatever we saw overwhelmed us absolutely and I for one came away ruminating on the various ingenious ways that rich and powerful men have employed over the ages in order to defy or deny death and erect elaborate pretences to assert that they would continue to rule in the afterlife too.

Shanghai was another experience where amidst impressive modern structures the old architecture survived in pockets of the city. We were taken to a 'village' in the suburbs where the old cobblestone streets and the old-fashioned houses were preserved as national monuments. In certain sections of this village only cycles were allowed to ply. Walking through the streets in Shanghai was also an example of the old and the new co-existing amidst the sea of humanity where street vendors sold hand-made mementos in the shade of high-rise edifices. The one other thing I must mention is the culinary delights we sampled wherever we went in China. The attraction of the table was such that even a non-pork-eater ventured to do what all Chinamen do in China!

The other trip sponsored by Sahitya Akademi was to participate in the London Book Fair. Apart from the back-breaking, feet-swelling coverage of the Fair grounds itself where we rushed about to listen to famous writers at different venues there, we were taken to suburban bookstores for readings, and interactive sessions with local intellectuals. From my trip to Derbyshire on such a jaunt, what has stayed in my mind is the exquisite and peaceful beauty of the English countryside where life seemed to have retained its pristine harmony with nature. Talking about literature and about what we ourselves wrote in such surroundings was the most enchanting moments of my London trip. The environment itself created the harmonious atmosphere where it became immaterial whether any one of us was famous or not: what mattered was that we were all lovers of good literature and were reaching out to one another through our writing. One other foreign trip came my way when an international organization called Panos South Asia with a branch in Guwahati sponsored a few Naga artists and writers to visit Switzerland. We visited the museum at Basle which displayed a sizable number of Naga exhibits and where we participated in interactive sessions at the university there. We were then taken to Zurich for similar meetings. While there we went on day's visit to an icy peak called Mount Pilatos. It still takes my breath away when I remember the climb in the trolleys, the last leg of which was done in a huge glass elevator with a bunch of Japanese tourists. At a certain stage it looked as if we were going to crash against the icy cliff and the collective cry of horror that emanated from the crowd was something we would always remember in our nightmares. The top of the peak presented such a breathtaking yet forbidding scenario of snow-clad mountains that I was struck dumb: the only phrase that came to mind was 'terrible beauty'. All the surrounding mountains were cloaked in ice and in spite of the bright sunshine, it was bone-chillingly cold. And yet there was an unexplainable grandeur in the snowy mountains which made us seem so puny and insignificant in its presence. Later I thought that the icy spectacle reminded me of some scenes from a James Bond movie.

What I have learnt from my foreign trips are some hard facts about myself: that I am a die-hard 'stay-at-home' type and a true 'dehati' or 'gaolia' at heart! Away from India, at first everything looks bigger, better and shinier. But after the excitement at the novelty wears off, you realize that you are only one among a zillion travellers passing through and you begin to long for the little cottage you came from, the familiar food you ate and the language you spoke there. The 'temporariness' and the sense of not 'belonging' hits you with a bang and no matter how many photographs you click and how many souvenirs you manage to carry in your luggage, they will always remain 'not yours'. So each time I came back home, beginning from my trip to the USA, I returned a bit wiser, a bit more humbled and above all with a lot more acceptance of what I am, where I am and what I have. But then again, if someone offered me a free foreign trip now, my answer will surely be 'Why not?'

I still feel a little diffident to mention that I received the Padma Shri award from the Government of India in 2007, for Literature and Education, they said. I felt over-awed by the award then and if truth be told, still do. Then in 2009 I was given the Nagaland Governor's Award for Distinction in the field of Literature (as the citation reads). I cherish these awards and am grateful to the governments for bestowing this recognition however humble my contribution to either literature or education has been. I also accept the responsibility that goes with the recognition and am struggling to make the 'contribution' more meaningful and relevant to humanity at large.

Looking Back

When I look back on my thirty odd years of service with NEHU, I am amazed at the swiftness of the passage of years since that day in 1975 when I entered its portals as a very timid and unsure teacher. But now that I am retired and out of the rarefied university circle, I can see things with more objectivity. I now believe that my life has been richer for having spent them with the different batches of students over the years and the love and respect they have given me is my richest reward. I wish every single one of them the very best in life and thank them for having taught me that to be a good teacher, you need not be a brilliant academician, only a person with an understanding heart. And the other gift that I will always cherish is the enduring love and friendship of my colleagues who had sustained me during the darkest hours of my life and rejoiced with me when small achievements came my way a few times. May the Almighty bless them all and give them rewarding lives; a big *Khublei* to all those steadfast friends!

When I left NEHU for the last time, I was assailed once again by the feeling that I was 'losing' the 'home' that I had called my own these last thirty odd years and I carried that hollow feeling with me to my present 'home' in Dimapur. It took some doing to reconcile myself to the new circumstances and only now a sense of 'being at home' is beginning to settle in my mind.

Evolution of a Writer

I write this section with a sense of inadequacy and apprehension because I know that in comparison to many others who can lay claim to the appellation 'writer' I am as yet, only a pretender. My literary output is meagre, to say the least; yet I dare dream on and hence this section. In truth I cannot pinpoint any stage or period in my life when I consciously said to myself that I wanted to be a writer. Therefore I had to dig hard into the past to see what can, even remotely be connected to my present precarious status as a writer.

So let me go back to my High School days. As has been mentioned earlier, from this stage onwards, except the Assamese papers, all the subjects were taught in English and the exams too were conducted in this language. Sometime during the year in class VII, we were given an assignment to write a story/essay on the topic, 'I Am a Rupee Coin'. The teacher told us that we could write anything, all that she wanted to see was our ability to structure the sentences correctly and coherently. We were given two days to complete it and submit our papers to her. I do not remember exactly what my reaction to this task was, but on the appointed day I submitted my work. And I still remember the story I wrote about myself as a rupee coin. In the story the coin was mint-fresh and in the possession of a rich merchant. He used to go on business to other towns and cities frequently. One day, the servant who always accompanied him on these trips, found the master's coin purse lying on the table and he saw that one coin was almost slipping out of the open purse. Seeing the glinting coin, on an impulse, though he had never done anything like this before, the servant removed it and tucked it in the fold of his dhoti. That rupee coin was 'me'. The master did not notice anything amiss in a purse full of many other coins and as was the custom, master and servant set out, once more on another of their business trips. Somehow, I made the duo cross the Hooghly River in a row boat and while handling the oars, the servant's dhoti became loose and the coin slid from its folds into the waters. The story ended there with some words like 'I am now at the bottom of the river and will remain there forever'. The teacher must have liked the story because in our next class she read it out and smiled at me.

In another assignment when we were in class IX, we were told to write an account of any journey to a place of historical interest. I was in trouble; I had never been to any such place except to tea gardens with cousins and an obscure village in the Naga Hills. But I had to write the essay and hit upon a gamble. I told myself that I would describe an imaginary journey; but to where? After much agonizing, I said Agra and the Taj Mahal! But again, how? Then I said to myself, 'In a dream' and set about reading up on the monument, the possible routes and even invented a cousin who was paying my expenses. So I wrote the essay, quite convincingly, it seemed. The story however ended on a somewhat rude and jolting note. The last sentence went somewhat like this,

'When we came away, I heard the distinct sound of a conch shell being blown. Turning back I saw some people chasing an old sadhu out of the gates and I started to laugh. It was then that I woke up to find an old goat bleating beneath my bedroom window!' The teacher's response was somewhat muted but my classmates had a good laugh when the last sentence was read out. While I was doing my Diploma course at the CIEFL, Hyderabad I wrote another story as an assignment for the Literature paper which the teacher, Susie Tharu, liked and gave me an A for!

These were however stray incidents which I am perforce recalling now. I did not, at any point of time think that they could be of any significance as the starting point of the 'writer' lurking in me. It was poetry that my heart was set on from the very beginning. I used to scribble lines whenever something caught my imagination and I needed to express my thoughts. When I say beginning, I am referring mostly to my post-graduate days; perhaps my earlier life was too full of practical realities and did not allow for much introspection. Perhaps I did not need or think poetry then. But venturing out of the security of conventionality and having to cope with divergent pressures in a completely alien environment, I seemed to turn more and more to poetry to seek refuge from the contradictions of the life that I had opted for.

I began to make serious attempts at writing poetry only in the eighties when my life was defined now as a single parent with acute financial and other assorted problems Coupled with the struggle to keep the home fires going and trying to cope with the demands of my job, I also had to contend with an impossible emotional tangle. It was during such moments of internal turmoil that I often turned to poetry for succour; reading other poets and putting pen to paper to create some of my own. But in comparison to established poets, I thought my work was amateurish and even downright silly. It took me a long time to muster enough courage to show my work to anyone, let alone think of publishing it. However, the urge to be heard was very strong and before I ventured to approach any publisher, I timidly started reading the odd poem here and there in university circles and received encouraging responses from the audience. This bolstered my confidence in my writing and when I thought that I had enough 'finished' poems, I wrote to the late Prof. P. Lal of Writers' Workshop who readily accepted the bunch for publication. My first book of poems was thus published by him in 1988. It was called *Songs That Tell*. The second volume called *Songs That Try to Say* was also published by him in 1992. The third book of poems called *Songs of Many Moods* was published by Kohima Sahitya Sabha, Kohima, in association with Har-Anand Publications, New Delhi in 1995. The next one called *Songs from Here and There* was published by NEHU Publications, Shillong in 2003. Grassworks Books of Pune published the fifth book called *Songs From The Other Life* in 2007.

On the other hand, writing fiction was for me almost a fortuitous 'fluke'. It happened during a difficult period when I discovered that all inspiration to write poetry seemed to have evaoporated and I felt utterly devastated. I would agonize through sleepless nights; nights which had earlier helped me find the most memorable lines for my poems. Now they only seemed to mock at me, as though telling me that I had come to the end of the road and that the earlier outpourings were just a few 'flashes in the pan'. But something in me refused to accept this finality. So one day I stayed back in the Department long after everyone had gone and said to myself that if I could not write poetry, I would try fiction and began to compose a story. To my great surprise, I discovered that ideas simply flowed and before I knew, the outline of the story crystallized in my mind. I was jubilant and not willing to let the momentum slip away I started a different one at home. And so was born this writer of fiction and my first book of short stories *These Hills Called Home: Stories From A War Zone* published by Zubaan is the result of that forced excursion away from poetry! Encouraged by the reception of this book in reading circles, I continued to write some more stories which were published in a second book called *Laburnum For My Head* by Penguin.

A writer never feels that all is said or done yet, especially one like me who seems to have stumbled into the arena quite by accident. The road ahead is longer and more tortuous. In all honesty I can say that my road ahead is not always clear or smooth; I need to remind myself how far behind I am from all the runners ahead of me. Sometimes I confess I feel like the athlete who is caught doing only the first lap when the winner has already reached the finishing line! But I still scribble lines, compose story frames and spend the occasional sleepless nights and the struggle goes on. The rewards of being a writer are never monetary alone, though the odd cheque from publishers is a timely reminder that you ought to keep up the good fight! And there is the all-important question of genius; the sooner one accepts one's limitations as a writer, the better will be the going.

Being a famous writer, I believe, comes with a price and I often wonder what the big prize winners think when they receive the frenzied accolades of a Nobel or Booker or some other awards. Do they feel burdened with the expectations that go with the recognition? I am sure that they do because the reading public can often be unrelenting in their demands for a bestseller each time from such writers. And then sometimes one hears about the learned doubts: whether a particular book truly deserved the prize and such remarks sometimes lead to speculations about what goes into the politics of selection. Of course these are matters that tiny specks like me in the literary horizon can only observe from the periphery. Nevertheless, the fact remains that these special writers, too many to name here, are the luminaries in the visible rings of the literary universe whose works ignite our imagination and enthral us with the power of their genius. But the inherent beauty and scope of literature is such that within that universe there are countless other 'unsung' writers whose work can equally delight and inform.

As for peripheral writers like me, there is a definite sense of validation when I am told that some sections of my writing, be it poetry or fiction, have found a place in the syllabi of colleges and universities not only in the region but elsewhere in the country too; and the knowledge that some scholars are writing M.Phil and Ph. D theses on my poetry truly gives me the impetus to continue writing more, poetry of course, but now fiction too. Such interest in my work also makes me believe that what I write is relevant to the people and to life in general; and as a writer I feel that this is the most important ingredient in any writing: that literature be relevant to life.

I often ask myself this question: what has being a writer done to my life? The first practical answer would be: it has given me an excellent outlet to occupy my leisure after retirement. I feel that there is still some purpose in my life when I am picking away at my computer with one finger, even if the result quite often turns out to be awful poetry or insipid fiction! Still, I can say to myself, at least I am doing something! Not just lolling on the bed and spending endless hours before the idiot box! Pursuing a full-time vocation of writing has provided me with a novel way of occupying my time at this stage in my life when most of the struggles of my earlier life seem to be over and done with. This life also provides me with opportunities to keep in touch with other writers and poets from whom I can draw inspiration and gain insights into the world of other literatures and cultures. The intellectual energy generated through this pursuit in many ways also helps me to overcome the actual physical infirmities brought on by time! Mind over matter?

Truth be told, being considered a writer flatters me and I feel that in some way this validates my pretensions of being an intellectual! Who knows perhaps this was the recognition that I was groping for when I bungled through my married life in the most inexpert way. I used to think of myself then only as a frustrated housewife who was seeking something unattainable in life. And now I think that if only I could produce something more worthwhile than what I have been able to do so far, I am sure that my life-long striving for that extra dimension to my life will be somewhat vindicated. As for now, the vibrant sense of affirmation and legitimacy of the self that I have gained through writing is like coming a wee bit closer to the elusive pole-star I longed to touch through all my earlier strivings. It has been an uneven run and the race is still on.

In summing up, I have to admit that I have no illusion about the tenor and temper of the life that I have had. It has been wholly and totally an ordinary life comparable to others that one sees every day and in that sense this memoir is not going to be an earth-shaking or life-changing one. I have written this because, as I have explained in my Preface, I had to. What I have tried to do here is to say that it is the ordinariness of life that becomes so important to so many of us. It is the ordinariness that challenges us and pits us against enormous odds. From where I stand now, I can see the contours that this ordinariness has given to my life and how the challenges tested me in the crucible of my own failings and weaknesses. In this retrospective mood, I say this with a sense of awe, and even some pride that the rewards and joys of this ordinary life have far outweighed the hardships and heartaches. I can now look at myself without any shame or apology because I have fought the odds with the truth and integrity of my inner self and because of this, I am sure that when my children read this, they will be able to say, 'We understand you, mother'.

In this ordinary life the seemingly simple things like the love and care of parents and two square meals a day were the most important requirements. It was the absence of these in my childhood that made life so miserable and perhaps contributed to the fact that I grew up into maturity and motherhood with an inherent deficiency where I often failed to fulfil such emotional needs in those closest to me. If I have learnt anything from my life, it is this: it is the simple things of life like love, care and a kind word that make life worth living and adds that extra dimension to ordinariness. This truth has been summed up beautifully by the Australian poet Judith Wright in her poem called *Grace*, some lines of which are quoted below,

> *Life is a dailiness, a simple bread*
> *that's worth the eating...*
> *It seems to have nothing to do with things at all,*
> *require another element or dimension.*
> *Not contemplation brings it; it merely happens,*
> *past expectation and beyond intention...*
> *Maybe there was a word for it. Call it grace.*
> *I have seen it, once or twice though a human face.*

What better words than these to sum up the worth of a simple, ordinary life? And if anyone asks me now about mine, I will emphatically affirm, 'Yes, this ordinary life has been worth living because I received the *Grace* of many human hearts along the way'.